Wild Europe

Wild Europe

Exceptional places from Iceland to the Urals

Eric Brasseur & Erik Verdonck

With a foreword by Robert Macfarlane

F

FRANCES LINCOLN LIMITED

PUBLISHERS

CONTENTS

THE TONIC OF WILDNESS

'We need the tonic of wildness,' wrote Henry David Thoreau in 1854; 'We need to witness our own limits transgressed, and some life pasturing freely where we never wander.' Thoreau's cry, keen then, is urgent now. For we live in a world with a diminishing tolerance for the wild. The landscapes we inhabit and through which we travel have, increasingly, become disenchanted. Wildness in its most powerful forms – charismatic fauna, remote terrains – has been pushed to the margins, or cinched into pockets. The ecological history of Europe since the last Ice Age is almost wholly one of loss; the continent is troublingly haunted by the ghosts of its vanished species and its abolished landscapes.

Yet wild places do remain, here and there, scattered across the continent like an inland archipelago. *Wild Europe* maps that archipelago, and in doing so it creates a cartography of hope. For Brasseur's images prove not only how much we still have to lose, but also how much we gain from our encounters with the wild. The glimpses he gives us – of eagle, wolf, bear and orca, of glacial ice, deep swamp, wildwood and canyon-land – jolt the mind and heart as well as the eye. They remind us that to experience wildness is often to be changed as a person; to be left ethically and spiritually reshaped in ways that are difficult to articulate, but unmistakable to feel.

Together, Brasseur and Verdonck have produced a deeply knowledgeable and beautiful book, which should be read partly as a warning but mostly as a celebration. *Wild Europe* is the work of two men who are both gluttonously hungry for the wild, and both passionate in their belief that – as Thoreau put it – 'what is wild' is 'near to what is good'.

Robert Macfarlane

THE INSTINCT TO EXPLORE

For me it all began in the Ardennes, at my grandparents' home: their garden, the forest of Anlier near by, an impression of the primeval forest and the river Sûre. The animals, the plants, the riverbanks, the birds and the dragonflies colour my memories. And the scent of the forest continues to enchant me. That mysterious life, nature, is still a continuous source of inspiration for me today. It is the well where I can quench my thirst, inexhaustibly. For the photographer it presents a challenge of a metaphysical nature, for don't those kinds of places surpass our imagination?

I walk alone through the river of life, trying to observe ever more sharply and always hoping to experience the ultimate moment: symbiosis with nature. Contemporaries whom I admire showed me how to do this: Robert Hainard, Jean Malaurie, Nicolas Bouvier and Paul Géroudet, artists and their predecessors. The book you are reading is the result of a voyage of discovery to exceptional places, a journey with many diversions, lasting many years.

But many things cannot be illustrated, simply because they are of another order. I am thinking, for instance, of my meeting out at sea with a killer whale, who surfaced from the water and looked at me with a critical eye. Or a young wolf among the ferns in a dense forest who took one glance at me and promptly decided to take to his heels. Or the trembling hind with whom I stood eye to eye on one of the forlorn peaks of the Highlands: I thought she was hurt, but in fact she had just brought her fawn into the world.

In such 'wild' areas, meetings with humans can also be stunning, just as some landscapes are. For instance, in the Russian steppe I met a Cossack woman who was hunting wolves with her super-fast Borzoi greyhounds. I followed bird ringers in the treetops, learning their technique and discovering the climber hidden in each of us. In Scotland for several days I was the guest of international high society in a castle in the middle of the Highlands.

The Ural mountains are a journey to the other side, where faces speak of two worlds, Europe and Asia. The Balkans stir the soul with their music. The labyrinth of the Berezina swarms with mosquitoes; no wonder the partisans there managed to escape from the Germans in 1945. The Finnish taiga at a temperature of minus 35°C was the worst ordeal – a place where the stakes can be high. Getting lost in a primeval forest will always be an adventure recalling primitive fears.

But in the end it is only the journey that counts.

Eric Brasseur

Continental Europe has five big carnivores – the wolf, the wolverine, the brown bear and the Eurasian and the Iberian lynx. The preservation of these animal species is a great challenge in a densely populated continent. These major predators need a great deal of room, between 100 and 1,000 km² per individual. Young animals often travel across hundreds of kilometres. The populations remain small – 0.1 to 3 individuals per 100 km². Only very few protected nature reserves have enough room to accommodate more than a few of each animal. Moreover, cohabitation between large carnivores and man remains problematic. This requires active management – reintroduction, relocation, control of hunting – and continual consultation with all parties living and working in and on the zone involved.

Source: IUCN (International Union for the Conservation of Nature)

WILD DREAMS

Imagine a continent without motorways and airports, without towns and frontiers. Imagine a wilderness that has escaped the hand of man. Pure and virgin. With endless woods, green plains enclosed by walls of mountains, wild rivers that carry water unhindered to the sea. A continent that lives by the rhythm of the seasons. Where everything is part of an ecosystem, where the links of the chain are still intact. Where the frogs that feed on insects and larvae themselves fall prey to armies of storks. Where wolves single out the weakest deer of the herd and tear it apart. Where fungi, larvae and insects flourish in and on the rotting wood of fallen trees . . .

Primeval Europe

I look at a relief map of Europe and see a large green patch squashed between mountainous spines in the far north, the south and the east. In the west is the blue ocean, scattered with islands that hover between Europe and America. But 'Where might there still be a real wilderness in Europe?' wonders my friend, the photographer Eric Brasseur. We bend over the great relief map, and slowly this project takes shape; with some hesitation we plant the first flags. We think about the orcas and sea eagles in northern Norway; Iceland, a geological laboratory; the boundless Highlands; the Azores; the small dots in the Atlantic Ocean where sperm whales show their tails and, we hope, a little more; bears and wolves in the Italian Abruzzi; the last European bison in the Polish forests; the mysterious wolverines, also known as gluttons, in Finnish Lapland . . . Gluttons, that's what we are. We want to cover everything, go everywhere, walk for days through inaccessible places and above all discover where primeval Europe hides itself. We make a first, rough, travel plan. Soon our scrawls are faxed through in all directions. Eric rouses his slumbering network of park rangers, biologists, nature lovers and experts. We make contact with a publisher.

A good photograph must be earned

We soon realize that Eric has actually been working on this project for years. Think of his trips to the swamps of Berezinski in Belorussia, or the months he spent tracking in the Highlands – among all his journeys still his favourite. Eric walks about and observes with the keen eye of a natural-history expert. He wants to feel the environment, to conquer the heights and the climate. A good photograph has to be earned, he believes. Without means, but with the help of local park rangers – sometimes, heaven help him, even from huntsmen – he goes looking for bears in Slovenia or wild bison in Poland, with oceans of patience and without any guarantee of success. 'It was a week before I caught sight of the bison, and even then it was just for a very short moment,' he recalls. Sometimes his brave attempts end in nothing. In the Carpathians in Poland he found many animal tracks but couldn't actually observe the animals, who kept themselves secret, just as the wildcat does on the flanks of Etna in Sicily. Animals are, after all, shy in areas where there is a great deal of hunting close to their habitat; it is in their own interest to be so. When bears go too close to a village they will get shot at. I think back to a trip we did together to the Lofoten islands in northern Norway. We went there to see the orcas. I stayed for a week and did not see a single one. Eric stayed on for another week and saw sixty of them. The herring that overwinter

ANNICK SCHNITZLER

PROFESSOR OF FOREST ECOLOGY AT THE UNIVERSITY OF METZ

There is no true wilderness in Europe. Everywhere the pressure of people is felt, who want to manage nature for their own good. So the forest has to be productive (forestry, hunting, tourism...). We are far removed from the primeval forest in which man once had his place alongside the plants and animals. There are in Europe actually still regions where elements of wilderness have been preserved. It is all important that such areas are protected and, wherever possible, nature is given a chance to recover itself. There is, for instance, a zone of 300 km² in Sardinia which is no longer exploited. If all goes well, there should be a new primeval forest there in two hundred years time. There are very beautiful natural regions in Europe, regardless of the level of integration of man. The condition for the restoration of ecosystems – and biodiversity – is respect for the natural processes.

in the fjords and attract the orcas had delayed swimming into the fjords because the water was still too warm. If one small link gets stuck, the chain breaks.

How much longer?

Europe is not a safari park. But even if you miss that one hoped-for, ultimate sighting, the journey will be worth the effort. To track down animals and observe them is detective work, and that is what makes it so thrilling. Moreover, you experience the enormous variety of the patchwork quilt that is Europe. We might almost forget that there are glaciers here, and geysers, tundra, volcanoes, canyons, archipelagoes, primeval forests and a pin-prick of desert. We are so estranged from nature that we can only dream of it. Yet the wilderness really exists, even on the old continent with its 500 million inhabitants. But for how long?

The economy has to grow; our never-abating hunger gnaws at the planet. The last remnants of wilderness seem like the concern of enthusiastic romantics who have not moved with the times and who have withdrawn from the daily battle for progress.

Nevertheless, awareness is growing that people are in fact part of nature. It is in our interests to look after the environment. The survival of our planet depends on it. We are confronted with scenarios of doom resulting from global warming and other disturbances of the environment in which man has had a hand. There are also positive signs. For instance, Europe is calling for part of its area to be reserved as 'wilderness'. Eric Brasseur and I hope this will be the case for a number of areas that he has visited. These areas are often inaccessible, unsuitable for human habitation. In any case a massive onrush would affect the ecosystem irrevocably, and lead to the disappearance of rare plants and animals. These areas, therefore, remain places to dream of – and this book will help you to do that.

Erik Verdonck

FACTS & FIGURES

Europe is one of the most fragmented continents, where for thousands of years man has put a heavy pressure on the environment. The result is a mosaic of semi-natural habitats. Only 1 per cent of the land area comes under the heading 'wilderness', in particular the primeval forests in Scandinavia, Poland and Russia. Conservationists are now trying to connect important habitats with each other via 'green corridors', or ecological networks, along which species can migrate; and 17 per cent of the land surface of the EU countries comes under the Pan-European Ecological Network (PAN parks) and Natura 2000. Conservation is more than ever essential. More than 700 animal species are at the moment under pressure in Europe, including 43 per cent of the bird species. Between 1990 and 2000 the greatest decline in the whole of Europe was in peat, marsh, coastal and heathland regions. The number of woods and lakes increased, but that increase can be discounted by the greatest habitat expansion: that of the industrial and built environment. The decline of a number of common birds continues. The number of butterflies, amphibians and insects that are important for pollination has also declined.

Source: IUCN (International Union for the Conservation of Nature)

Population pressure is the greatest problem for the environment in Europe and the world.

Jean-Claude Genot

THE LAST WILDERNESS OF EUROPE

Jean-Claude Genot is an ecologist in heart and soul. He is responsible for the management of the nature reserve Les Vosges du Nord, where he oversees sustained forestry management. Genot travels a great deal, particularly in eastern Europe. Consequently he has a good picture of the ecosystems in Europe. 'It's hard to find any really virgin nature in Europe now,' says Genot. 'Man's presence is everywhere, or else he has left his spoor behind. Take the Scottish Highlands, generally considered to be a piece of wilderness. It was once an area covered in forests, but thanks to the activities of man the forests have disappeared. Moreover, the Highlands have for centuries been intensively grazed by sheep.' After the last Ice Age, 10,000 years ago, Europe was largely covered with forest. Since we enjoy a moderate climate here, forest became the primeval environment of the continent. But through human activities that forest too has now largely disappeared. 'Man is the only being capable of deforestation,' says Jean-Claude Genot. 'Recently we followed the tracks of twenty-two bison in Białowieża in Poland. We could hardly hear them. A single man would have done more damage.' As the ecological footprint of man has grown larger, the forest has disappeared. The wilderness has shrunk dramatically.

Wild means rich

France has 16 million hectares of forest – twice as much as at the end of the nineteenth century, but only one third of the original forested area. Moreover, the planted forest is much less dense (200 m³ per hectare) than the earlier primeval forest (500 m³ per hectare). If the density is taken into account, France now has 90 per cent less forest than it did originally. Primeval forest is essential for a healthy ecosystem. In primeval forest there are thousands of plant and animal species, sometimes distributed over hundreds of hectares, as in Poland. The forest continually renews itself. In and around dead tree trunks (which you barely find in young, planted woods), insects, larvae and worms abound. That

is where the majority of the indigenous biodiversity is hidden. 'Together with WWF France I set up the "Forêts Sauvages" project, explains Jean-Claude Genot. 'We buy up estates and leave them to run wild. In this way we want to invest in the environment for the future, and in biodiversity.' Forêts Sauvages is a national initiative, which has also purchased land in the Haute Loire and the valley of the Allier.

Freedom

Everyone has a right to a free environment, Genot believes. 'Today all nature is subject to restraints, imposed by the hand of man. Where can you still walk undisturbed for days, camp in the open air or enjoy the silence of the forest? Man dominates nature, and that smells of dictatorship. Our relationship with nature is problematic, but we don't want to admit it. For us nature is everything "that is not human". But we should admit that we, too, are mammals and that we are not outside nature. It is important that people determine what relationship they want with nature, and to what extent they are prepared to let nature be free. The more we give in to our obsession with managing everything, the more we will realize that we don't actually control anything. Civilization means that you leave room for nature. Without nature we can't live. Concrete towns make people unhappy and encourage conflict. For many youngsters the computer is the gateway to a virtual world, yet how will they later deal with nature? Does progress have to mean that nature disappears?' Jean-Claude Genot pleads for education on nature. If you want to enjoy nature, he says, take the trouble to find out about it. The wilderness offers a unique experience. There, where natural thresholds – altitude, climate, water – hinder exploitation, is where nature defends itself best. It is no coincidence that the greatest wilderness in Europe is in the north and east. Elsewhere the pressure of population is much greater. But the real 'wild Europe' does not exist. Man is (and has been) everywhere. 'It does not stop us dreaming,' Genot says. 'Show ten people the same

JEAN-CLAUDE GENOT

The Frenchman Jean-Claude Genot gained his doctorate in Ecology at the University of Burgundy, studied organic chemistry at the Louis Pasteur University in Strasbourg and became a chemical engineer at the Ecole Nationale Supérieure de Chimie de Strasbourg. Since 1982 Genot has been environmental engineer in the Parc Naturel Régional des Vosges du Nord in France. He takes an active role in Unesco's Man and Biosphere programme, particularly in Berezinski in Belorussia, a park he has visited sixteen times. Genot is the author of several publications about nature and the preservation of the environment on behalf of Unesco and the Council of Europe. He has written extensively about birds in French and foreign magazines, and has devoted himself particularly to the study of the little owl.

landscape and you will get ten different impressions. Everyone experiences it from their own point of view, their own background and their own emotions. Personally I have a need for my own ration of virgin nature – a physical and mental need. When I take a walk through the forest, I want to feel the wind on my skin. I like to walk, to explore, to go off the beaten track. During such a walk I enjoy the peace of observing, of the smell and sound of the wood.'

Homo disparitus

The environment can recover itself remarkably quickly. Take the disaster at the nuclear reactor at Chernobyl in the Ukraine in 1986. All human activity was stopped within a radius of 30 kilometres. Butow bears, eagles, wild boar and wolves have again been seen there. In his book, *Homo disparitus*, Alain Weisman paints a picture of an environment that restores itself in areas where people have been absent for some time, such as the frontier areas between North and South Korea, or between Turkish and Greek Cyprus. An example nearer home is a green corridor in the area where the Iron Curtain used to separate the East from the West. In the narrow strip of wood there are unique animal and plant species. There are now movements to protect the whole corridor, from north to south. 'The environment has a future if people put themselves in a modest position, and allot themselves a place in nature, and not outside it,' believes Jean-Claude Genot. We are part of the living organism that is Earth. We have every interest in keeping this system in balance. A society succeeds only when it adapts itself to its environment. We are estranged from nature, but we still need it.'

Questions

Wild Europe considers the relationship between people and nature within Europe. We are looking for an answer to the question of why exactly an ecosystem has survived. Was it once a sacred wood, the hunting domain of a royal family, a tsar? Was it intended for hunting and therefore purged of predators? Why did the environment stay intact? Wherever man has involved himself with nature, he has left his track behind. Where he has stopped felling trees, the environment has developed freely again. This book asks questions. What part is played by the wild environment and what has been influenced by man in this landscape? Why is this environmental region exceptional? To what extent is it really wild? The wilderness can express itself in various ways, on a varying scale. Nature is never homogeneous. When it is not forced by man into the restrictions of homogeneity, nature diversifies. That is why some trees react differently to the same environmental factors. The primeval forest will regenerate spontaneously after a storm. In a planted wood the damage is often much greater.

Man and nature are complementary, like light and shadow. Wild nature alerts us to our humanity. Wild nature makes us humble and teaches us how to defend ourselves. 'I am glad that there is a wilderness I can dream about,' says Jean-Claude Genot. 'In this way I escape from the omnipresent alarm clock, mobile phones, computer . . . Nature offers us the chance to oppose the dictatorship of man over the planet. What bliss it is to be able to walk through the woods without the compulsion of the mobile phone.'

Forest is the queen on the chessboard, the piece that should dominate in nature, and should develop spontaneously everywhere.

Robert Hainard, Swiss animal artist, etcher and sculptor

Europe's vegetation

A journey through Europe reveals a great variety of landscape and vegetation. Around the Mediterranean grow forests of umbrella pines or evergreen woods of holm oak; during a walk in the Ardennes one is surrounded by large beech forests; in Scandinavia there is a sea of coniferous trees, while in the true far north the views are uninterrupted because of the lack of trees in the landscape. During a trip from the Alpine valleys to the tops of the Alps the same landscapes appear, from beech woods to coniferous forest to heath and grasslands, up to bare rocks and snow and ice.

The vegetation of Europe can be classified into five zones, listed here from north to south. The average annual temperature determines the zone.

Tundra

In the far north of Europe no trees grow. In many places the ground thaws only on the surface in the summer. Deep down the subsoil stays frozen all through the year. The vegetation has to grow in a period of barely two months, which is too short for trees. The tundra is therefore a world of herbs, small shrubs, rocks, mosses and lichen, where herds of reindeer have to find their food. This is where the mysterious snowy owl is at home.

Taiga

In slightly longer summers some birches and particularly coniferous trees manage to survive. Coniferous trees can photosynthesize even at low temperatures, so they dominate in this region. The endless northern taiga covers a large part of Scandinavia and the northern half of Russia south of the tundra. The three most important species of trees are the spruce, the Scots pine and the birch. The silver fir and the larch also occur. The woods are interrupted by lakes, marshes and fens, which are possible because the cold climate prevents rapid evaporation. Cranes and capercaillies breed in these regions.

The deciduous woodland zone (or nemoral zone)

Deciduous trees take over from coniferous trees when the growing season (i.e. when average temperatures are higher than 10°C) lasts for longer than four months. The summer-green deciduous woodland zone extends across central Europe, from the British isles to the Urals, via France, Germany, Poland, Belorussia and Russia. In the north of this zone maples, ashes, limes, summer oaks and beeches as well as spruces make up the woods. Farther south, coniferous trees disappear and the appearance of the woods is determined by deciduous trees. These trees lose their leaves during cold and therefore dry winter conditions, which are unsuitable for photosynthesis. In the primeval forest, rich in dead wood, the collared flycatcher and the white-headed woodpecker breed. When these deciduous woods are not disturbed by man, they make one of the most biodiverse landscapes and provide a habitat for large predators such as the bear, the wolf and the lynx.

The sub-Mediterranean (or thermonemoral) zone

As you go south the summers get increasingly warmer, although it still freezes regularly during winter. The trees adjust themselves: they still always drop their leaves in winter, but the leaves become thicker, leathery and often very hairy underneath, so that in summer they lose less water through evaporation. The western part of this area has beautiful woods of Pyrenean oak, downy oak, sweet chestnut and Hungarian oak. There are a few species of pine: the Austrian pine, the Corsican pine and the maritime pine. The booted eagle circles above the sun-drenched flanks of the mountains and on the edge of the oak wood the eastern Bonelli's warbler sings of the advent of summer. Farther to the east it is dryer. Steppe replaces the forest, from Moldavia to the Caspian Sea. The steppe eagle hunts the spotted suslik and the great bustard parades there in spring.

The Mediterranean zone

Here it hardly freezes in winter. The trees keep their leaves in winter and the dry summer encourages the growth of trees with small, leathery leaves, such as the cork oak, the holm oak, the ilex, the olive and the mastic. There are also several kinds of coniferous trees: the umbrella pine, the Aleppo pine, the Italian cypress. In the warmest parts of this area grows the palmetto, the only wild palm in Europe. As night falls, the Scops owl breaks the silence with its unique screech. At the first light of dawn the swelling chatter of the Sardinian warbler resounds.

IDENTIFYING FACTORS

1. Think about the plant species described above and you will easily recognize the vegetation zone in which you find yourself. They are dominant or easily recognizable species that determine the appearance of the natural landscape.

2. The natural vegetation has been radically changed by man through agriculture and forestry. It may well happen, for instance, that you travel through immense spruce woods but that you are not in the taiga at all: you may be in the Ardennes, where these trees were planted to replace the deciduous beech wood. Observation teaches us that planted trees are often all of the same age and arranged in straight lines. Here and there some beeches have survived, with young beech or other deciduous shrubs in the undergrowth.

3. There is a strong similarity between the large vegetation zones measured by degree of latitude throughout Europe and the vegetation zones measured by increase in height of the European mountain ranges. If you travel from Provence to the top of the Alps you cross through a lowland level with holm oak (Mediterranean), then a hilly zone with downy oak (equivalent to the warm, temperate zone of deciduous woods), a mountain zone with beech (temperate zone of deciduous woods), a subalpine zone with Norway spruce and larch (taiga) and, finally, a zone of dwarf shrubs, an alpine meadow with a wealth of herbs and dominated by grass (together equivalent to the tundra). This – admittedly not perfect – connection can be explained by the fact that the average annual temperature drops by half a degree per 100 metres altitude, just as half a degree per 100 kilometres is lost towards the north. To put it simply, 100 metres in altitude has the same effect as 100 kilometres to the north.

4. Local conditions can create various islands with differing vegetation within the dominant type. Slopes facing a different direction sometimes have a different climate – a microclimate. For instance, in a beech zone you may often find a downy oak on hills facing south. On the chart below you will find boundaries that are valid for average local conditions (flat, normal subsoil). In reality you will always first meet islands of the next type when you approach a transitional area between two zones. These islands become larger and connect more closely;

then the zone you are leaving falls apart into islands which gradually become smaller and farther away from each other. In the same region an average annual temperature that is one degree higher than the norm is measured on a slope facing south; a northerly slope gives two degrees less. These differences between orientation to the south and the north equal 600 metres difference in altitude or 600 kilometres distance between south and north (measured in Central Europe).

5. Within a vegetation zone you can distinguish subdivisions measured by the average temperature (from north to south) by the increasing continental character in an eastern direction – more humid and less extreme (Atlantic) climate in the west, dryer (continental) climate with more contrasting temperatures in the east – and by the type of subsoil (acid or lime).

6. Average annual temperature per vegetation zone (median Europe):

Vegetation zone	Average annual temperature
TUNDRA	below 0° C
TAIGA	from 0 tot 5° C
NEMORAL ZONE	from 5 tot 10° C
THERMONEMORAL ZONE	from 10 tot 14° C
MEDITERRANEAN ZONE	from 14 tot 20° C
TROPICAL ZONE (outside Europe)	higher than 20° C

The difference in temperature is slightly higher in the west (because of milder winters) than in the east.

7. Some vegetation types escape this climatologically defined classification: so-called azonal vegetation. This is vegetation on particular types of soil or exposed to extreme circumstances, such as being on the edge of the sea, in estuaries or in freshwater environments (lakes, marshes, rivers).

Source: P. Ozenda, Végétation du continent européen, Delachaux et Niestlé, 1994

North Cape

ARCTIC OCEAN

⑧

①

⑨

Scandinavian Mountains

Lapland

Sweden

Finland

Norway

Iceland

⑤

ATLANTIC

OCEAN

North Sea

Denmark

Baltic Sea

Estonia

Latvia

Lithuania

⑱

⑭

⑫

⑪

⑭

Belorussia

Ireland

United Kingdom

The Netherlands

Germany

Poland

Belgium

Luxembourg

Czech Republic

Slovakia

Carpathian Mountains

Moldavia

France

Austria

Hungary

⑬

Liechtenstein

⑩

Switzerland

The Alps

Slovenia

⑳

Romania

San Marino

⑥

Adriatic Sea

Croatia

Bosnia and Herzegovina

⑲

Massif Central

Monaco

Serbia

Pyrenees

Montenegro

Bulgaria

⑫

Andorra

Vat.

Italy

Kosovo

②

Portugal

Spain

⑦

Macedonia

④

③

Albania

Sierra Morena

⑮

Greece

Azores

ATLANTIC OCEAN

Madeira

Portugal

Mediterranean Sea

⑳

Sicily

Malta

Morocco

Algeria

Tunisia

POLSKA

BIALOWIEŻA · BIEBRZA · WOLINSKI · KARPATY

BIALOWIEŻA – LOWLAND PRIMEVAL FOREST

BISON IN THE FOREST

'I am surrounded by enormous, centuries-old oaks – as many as 800 trees that are more than 300 years old,' I scrawl in my diary. I move silently through the marsh. There is a heavy, dull sound. Unexpectedly the dark mass of two bison looms. Hidden in a cloud of mosquitoes and horseflies, I watch these two great grazers with fascination. From a distance I see a mammal I don't know. No, it's not a wolf, nor a wolverine . . . The animal moves slowly, rather inelegantly, and dissolves into nothing. Just like the bison, which have vanished in a flash. Is this a dream or reality? The camera film will tell us. The hammering of a black woodpecker echoes in the woods, the only sound in an ocean of silence.

In the village the stork reigns. There is at least one of these stilt-walkers on each roof. The sound of their clattering fills the air. Opposite a farm is the largest storks' nest in Poland. A couple of greater spotted eagles circle high above me. The hunt for pictures can begin now.

Białowieża

Białowieża in eastern Poland and in western Belorussia is one of the last great primeval forests in the European lowlands. On the Polish side there are about 10,000 hectares of forest, in Belorussia 77,000 hectares. It is not the largest European forest area, but it is one of the least impaired. In 1932 the reserve acquired the status of national park. In 1947 this area of natural beauty was recognized by Unesco as a biosphere reserve. The primeval forest remained untouched because the Polish kings and Russian tsars used it for hunting. Most trees were preserved, but the wolves and the European bison became extinct. The wild European bison died out as early as 1919 and was reintroduced ten years later.

In the park you will find all the important tree species: spruce, oak, lime, maple, aspen, birch. The presence of the spruce – one of the most important species in the park – and of the plants and animals that live in perfect symbiosis with it gives the ecosystem a special character. The wood lies in the transitional area between the boreal and the temperate zones and is a last witness to what once was a primeval forest in the lowland. There are several tree species present at the limit of their area of distribution: the Norway spruce reaches the southern boundary of its spread here, and the durmast oak its north-eastern limit. The wood is like a mosaic of oak-lime-hornbeam and pine-spruce-oak.

There is no 'tidying up' here. Bare, diseased and dead trees remain standing among living ones; after a while they fall over, or break up and then provide food for moulds and insects. On the bark colourful fungi grow, as well as ferns and mosses, and rare wood sorrel. Young rowan trees flourish, particularly on partly decayed tree trunks. The fauna in this virgin forest is particularly rich and includes around 12,000 species, of which most are invertebrates. About 120 different bird species nest here, and there are 54 species of mammals, 7 species of reptiles and 11 species of amphibians.

BISON

Is there a difference between the European and the American bison? There are two kinds of bison: the prairie bison and the wood or mountain bison of Athabasca, Canada. European bison show a strong resemblance to the latter. They differ from the American prairie bison in the thickness of their coat and in their horns. European bison have round horns (because of the branches in the forest); American prairie bison have straight horns. Both species are more or less the same size. In the past the European bison lived throughout Europe in deciduous woods and mixed woodland. In the early twentieth century the only European bison (also known as wisent) left were to be found in Białowieża. A Caucasian subspecies lived in the mountains of that name. During the First World War the species in Białowieża became extinct, but those in the Caucasus managed to survive. Now there are about 550 bison in the Polish part of Białowieża and 350 in the Belorussian part. You can still find wild European bison in Poland in Borecka, Knyszyńska, Walcz and the Bieszczady mountains, and in Belorussia, Russia, Lithuania, Ukraine and Slovakia. At the moment there are about six animals for every 10 km² (about 1.5 km² per animal). Bison are grazers. They feed on grasses (70–90 per cent), branches, bark and leaves of trees and shrubbery (10–20 per cent). They eat up to 400 different plant species, including fungi, lichen, mosses and oakapples.

▶ *An evocation of Bison bonasus.*

INTERVIEW WITH CONSERVATIONIST CZESLAW OKOLOW

Why is Białowieża an exceptional ecological location?
Białowieża is the best-preserved natural lowland forest in Europe, unique in the boreal zone. You will find an enormous biodiversity there, both in vegetation and in fungi, moulds and animals.

What are the natural enemies of the European bison living in the wild?
Originally they were the wolf and the brown bear. There are now no bears left in Białowieża, but occasionally wolves hunt the bison successfully.

What could threaten the bisons' survival?
The most pressing concern is the fact that all the animals are the descendants of a mere thirteen bison which survived the First World War in captivity. Consequently there is very little genetic variety. Other threats are diseases such as foot-and-mouth disease, and the limited number of animals. We have only the one important population.

▼ Białowieża is an enormous green lung where you meet all the large predators. I also visited the closed and even more extensive Belorussian part.

▶ The heart of the forest remains untouched. Wilderness like this has disappeared from western Europe.

▶ This unique alluvial woodland has been a scientific laboratory for several decades.

▼ Inaccessible areas resound with noises, shrieks and buzzing insects.

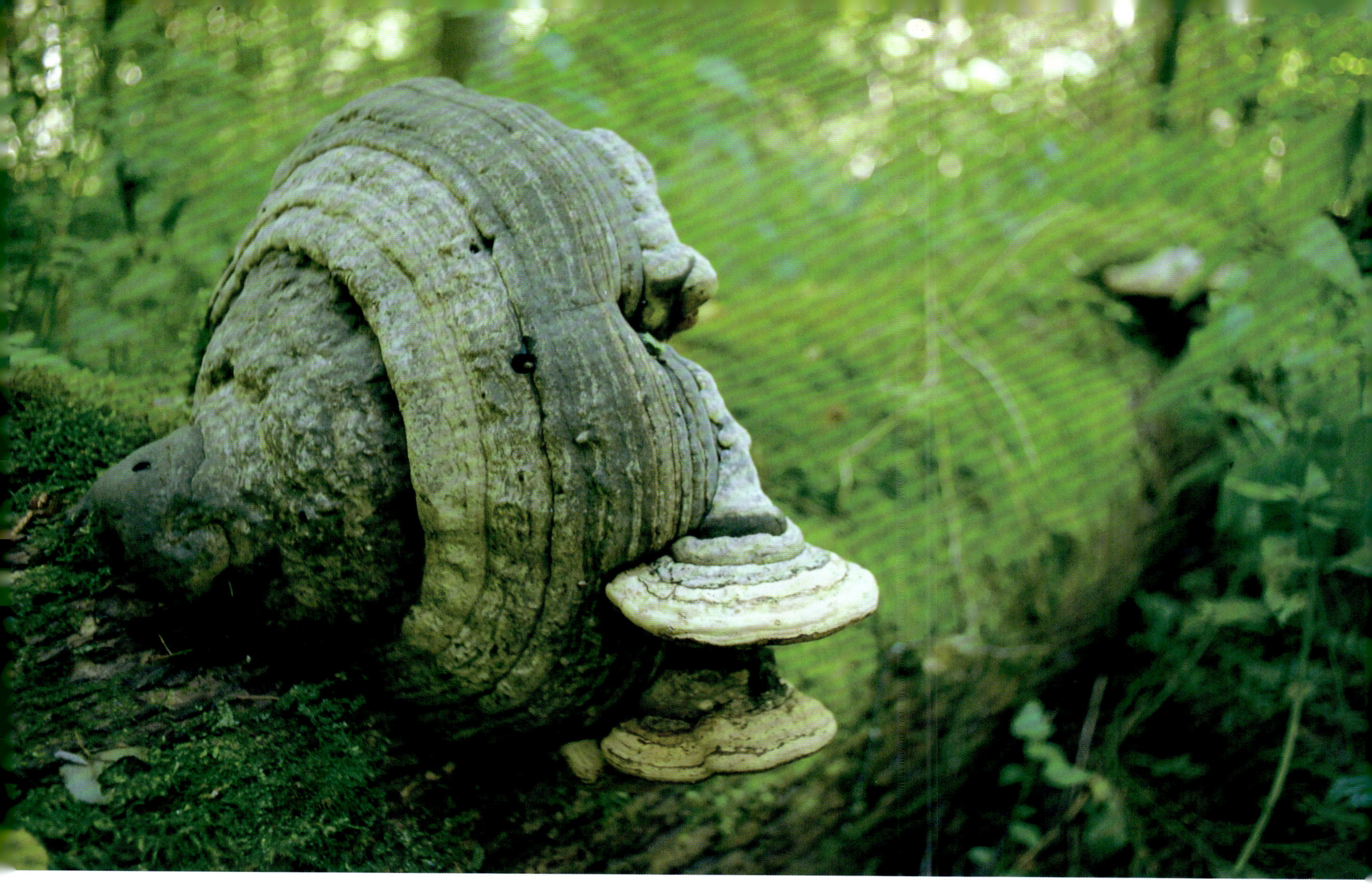
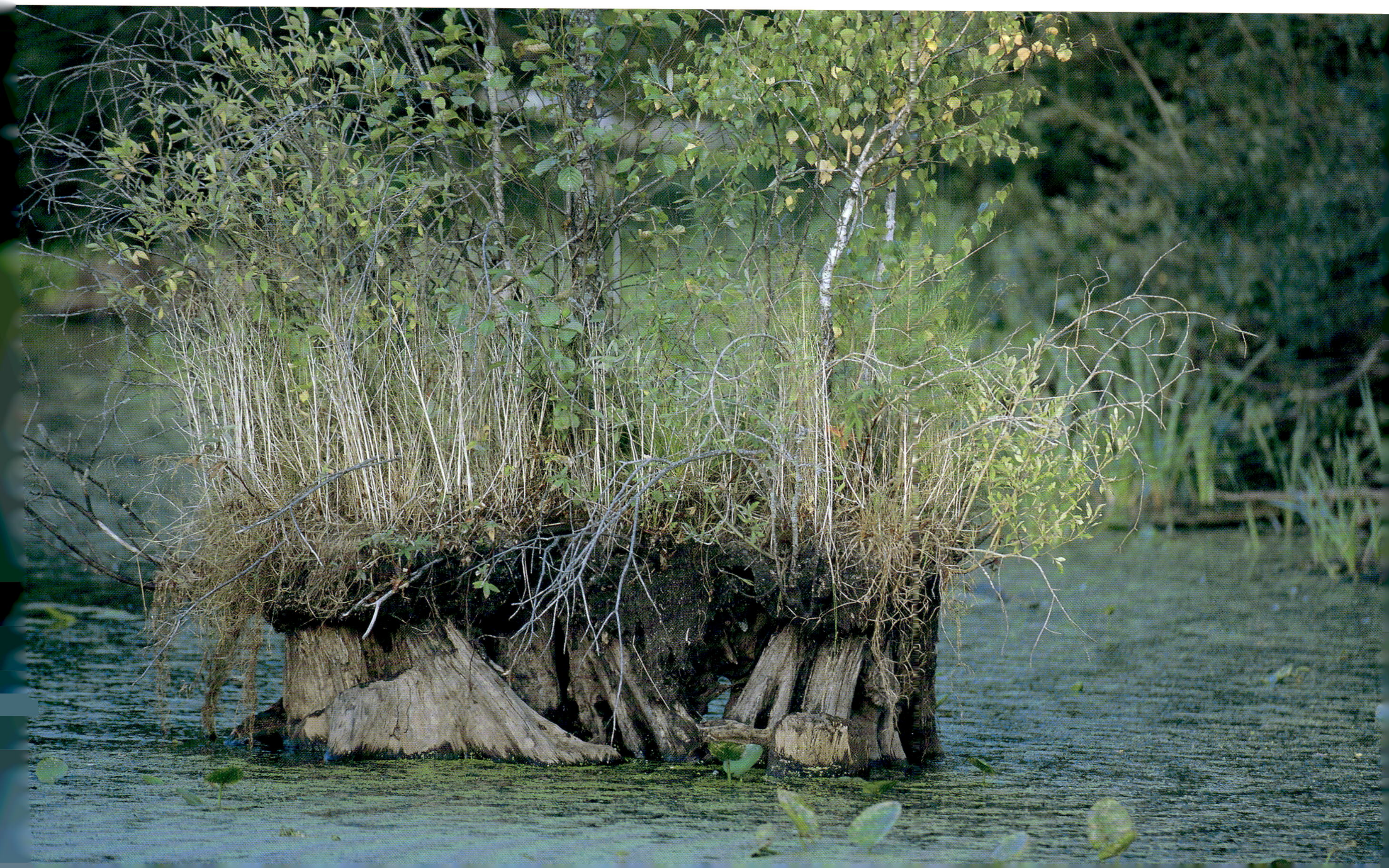

BIEBRZA – WET GRASSLAND, FENLAND AND MARSHES

PLAINS, FIELDS AND WATER

In front of me meanders the sublime Narew. Cows swim across to the far side of the river. The sky has turned black and white with storks, which hunt frogs, salamanders and fish. I have discovered a simple, pure area, full of poetry, which hovers between plain, field and water. A herd of wild horses rushes past; a buzzard and a sparrowhawk drink at a pool. I spot ospreys and swans. Mists appear and disappear. A lesser spotted eagle and a greater spotted eagle come and pay their respects. The largest marshland ecosystem of north-eastern Poland is once again full of elks. After the Second World War there was a keeper watching over each elk; now the elk is protected and the population is growing again.

Biebrza

The Biebrza National Park extends across marshlands along the banks of the Biebrza river and is characterized by very varied and often rare growth. The park is a true mosaic of running and still waters, old riverbeds and sandy ridges, reed and sedge fields, high moorland and low fenland, brushwood areas, shrubs and young trees, old forests and sparsely manured hayfields, with small villages along the edges and along the riverbanks.

The Biebrza National Park lies near the border with Belorussia. The Narew river and its confluence with the Biebrza make up the southern border. The park was set up in 1993. It is Poland's largest national park (59,233 hectares). It includes 15,547 hectares of woodland, 18,182 hectares of agricultural land and 25,494 hectares of wet grassland – the most important habitat, the well-known Biebrza marshes. Biebrza is a wetland of world importance and is protected by the Ramsar Convention. The area is unique in Europe because of its marshes, peat zones and diverse fauna, in particular its bird population.

The valley of the Biebrza has extensive peat bogs. After the glaciers receded, moraines formed and began an intensive transformation of plant remains into peat. The valley of the Biebrza in north-east Poland is now the largest relatively undisturbed peat-bog area in Europe. The river valley is 2 to 20 kilometres wide and has a total surface area of 90,000 hectares. The valley is unique because of the rather meandering Biebrza, a lowland watercourse with very clean water. The vast open wet grasslands, covered in sedge and various rare plants, are characteristic of this area, where 235 species of birds have been recorded.

INTERVIEW WITH A LOCAL CONSERVATIONIST, ARTHUR WIATR, OF THE BIEBRZA NATIONAL PARK

Why is Biebrza an exceptional area ecologically?
Biebrza is a very rare valley which is practically unspoilt and was saved from being drained. In the days of the tsars a few canals were dug, but the main river and the whole ecosystem stayed intact. For this reason Biebrza is seen as a model for lowland rivers where all natural processes occur, such as floods in spring. You can follow the complete life cycle of the river, and the fauna and flora are very rich and various.

Is there no human influence at all in the area?
Yes, there is human activity. For generations there has been extensive agricultural activity, with grazing by cattle and the traditional harvesting of hay. In this way the wet grasslands have been well maintained. Many rare birds found ideal conditions there for nesting, breeding, hunting and so on. Now farming has disappeared from the park, but the park remains responsible for its management – keeping the grass mown – in collaboration with the farmers, who are still the owners of the land.

What animals do you see here?
Biebrza is important for the reed warbler (it is the third largest area where these birds can find cover), the great snipe, the black grouse, the ruff, the white-winged black tern, the lesser spotted eagle and the greater spotted eagle. Among the mammals you will find large carnivores, such as the wolf, and big grazers, such as the elk. The elk population is the largest in Poland and in this part of Europe. There are also red deer, roe deer, beavers, otters and even a small number of lynx.

How do you view the evolution of Biebrza in the future?
Since Poland has joined the European Union a great deal has changed in agriculture and in the infrastructure of the area. These changes often carry with them threats to nature, the landscape and the architecture. Global warming can also have a negative influence on the park: shortage of water, for instance, threatens the indigenous fauna and flora. On the other hand we hope that European money will be used to counteract these threats.

Is Biebrza a model for nature conservancy in Poland and Europe?
Absolutely, particularly in respect of river management and the management of ecosystems in natural lowland rivers.

INTERVIEW WITH A FOREIGN CONSERVATIONIST, Luc Vanassche

Luc Vanassche, a Belgian, regularly visits Biebrza as part of a scientific cooperation programme. Luc is a forestry manager for the Flemish Agency for Nature and Forests.

Does Biebrza deserve the name 'wilderness'?

To tell you the truth, I am surprised you chose the Biebrza valley as an example of a wilderness in Europe. It is a valuable nature reserve, but it is certainly not a wilderness. In the past, man has put his stamp strongly on the entire valley. But in fact that has meant that a valuable and a special flora and fauna was able to develop. The national park was set up to protect this semi-natural biotope.

What is the history of the area?

Well into the late Middle Ages the use of the valley remained limited to hunting and fishing. Then the plateaux alongside the river valley were colonized and small villages built, and the vast deciduous forests were cut down to make room for pastures and arable farming. In the Biebrza valley itself much of the woods (elder and birch on boggy ground) was cut down too, so that the valley became a large, open peat area, covered with lush sedge vegetation which also contained many herbs and other plants. The sedge fields were cut in the summer, and sometimes grazed by cattle. Together with the increased intake of groundwater from the surrounding plateaux – where the woods that had held the water and allowed it to evaporate had disappeared – the cattle saw to it that shrubs and trees no longer had a chance to grow. Some alder and birch marshes were retained, but they were mostly used as coppice wood. So there was not much 'wilderness' to be found any more; even the narrow reed marshes along the river were mown regularly. Here and there the fenland was drained with a system of narrow, shallow ditches. In addition there was hunting. This explains why the elk was almost wiped out. And, particularly along the edge of the valley, peat was cut. From the 1960s onwards the tide turned: emigration meant that the population was drastically reduced and agriculture disappeared from the valley at an ever-increasing rate. Nowadays agriculture in north-east Poland has been almost entirely mechanized, and not a single farmer still mows the sedge fields in the peat bogs. There is also hardly any grazing in the actual fenland area; only downstream are there still quite a few cows and horses to be seen along the river in summer.

What influence has the disappearance of agriculture had on the environment?

The cessation of agricultural activity caused a 'secondary succession': open sedge vegetation was colonized by small shrubs and trees and there is now an evolution towards thickets of willow or alder or birch marshes. Whether this should be seen as a completely natural process is another question. One cannot forget the human input, in particular the drainage work of old canals and ditches. Climate change shows itself in reduced rainfall. We have found that the alder and birch coppices into which the former open fenland vegetation is being transformed are rather poor in their variety of species. In the course of time the biodiversity will probably increase, but at the moment this 'reforestation' is leading mainly to the disappearance of rare species of birds characteristic of Europe, such as the great snipe, the reed warbler, the short-eared owl, the Montagu's harrier and the hen harrier, the spotted crake, ruff, the common snipe, the greater spotted eagle and the lesser spotted eagle. The same goes for the characteristic species of butterflies such as the scarce heath, the small pearl-bordered fritillary and the large heath. Also in the forest areas the number of butterflies and plants is decreasing because of the loss of the earlier forms of management, such as cattle grazing in the forest and the management of coppices. Fortunately there are also species that benefit from this evolution. For instance, elks – which meanwhile have been declared protected – have increased significantly in numbers. Cranes can find breeding grounds more easily now, and the lynx have returned after a long absence. Yet the balance remains negative and that is why the national park wants to keep the characteristic open fenland area. Large areas of sedge marsh are now being mown with specially adapted machines.

Is there still a real 'wilderness' in Biebrza?

Certainly. Think of the almost 4,000 hectares of 'red' marsh of Czerwone Bagno, which was once created for the elk and has now developed for eighty years without any human intervention. Or the extensive marshy forest of Laskowiec, the Kapice forest with mainly alder. If you define 'wilderness' strictly as a 'large area which has had hardly any interference by man and everything develops according to natural processes', the Biebrza valley does not qualify, because it is man-made. But if you interpret it as a 'large area rich in diverse natural resources', the Biebrza valley certainly qualifies.

What does the future hold?

Unfortunately the relationship between man and nature is developing from a certain harmony to a division between man and nature characteristic of western Europe. Partly natural biotopes in the valley are becoming rougher and more forested, which could cause butter-flies, plants and birds to disappear. Around the valley, agriculture is changing fast: corn crops are developing, large tractors and harvesters are being used. This will lead to the disappearance of plants and animals that are linked to agricultural landscapes, such as the ortolan. Industrial agriculture will also threaten nature in the valley. Pesticides and manure will spread into the area via tributaries of the Biebrza or via groundwater streams, and will also flow into the fenland areas in the valley, and so contaminate it. The risk is that this will cause rare, critically important plants and animals to disappear and that 'overgrown' forests and neglect will manifest themselves even more strongly.

▲ A classic example of farming as it used to be done, without using pesticides.

▲ With its unusual body structure the elk is very well adapted to its biotope.

▲ The Tarpan horse, an old breed, has been reintroduced in the region.

▼ Cows wade through the slow-flowing stream of the Biebrza every day: a timeless scene.

WOLINSKI –
BALTIC COAST

TREES PLUNGING INTO THE SEA

Beaches without a shore, the largest shifting dunes of Europe, lashed by the harsh wind, and trees that plunge into the sea: those are my main impressions of the Baltic coast.

Wolinski

The Wolinski National Park is on the island of Wyspa Wolin. The landscape is very varied. It is made up of moraine hills – which dominate, covering about 75 per cent of the surface area of the park – post-glacial lakes and extensive beech woods. The cliffs in particular, up to 15 kilometres long and up to 95 metres high, are very striking. The altitude in the park varies from 0 to 115 metres. The island was formed when the sea wore away the coastal cliffs. The contours reflect the Scandinavian Ice Age of 12,000 years ago. The ice moraines are surrounded by younger, alluvial dunes and peat zones. To the west stretches a beach of fine sand with low sand dunes; to the east there are wooded hills that slope steeply down to the sea. The highest of these hills, Grzywacz (115 metres), is also the highest point of the entire Polish coast along the Baltic Sea. The park consists mainly of the higher, central, sloping part of the island, which runs down to the sea in the north and to the Szczecin Bay in the south. The long Wolin cliffs are only a fragment of the 45 kilometres of active cliffs along the Baltic coast. The landscape is subject to continual change. Storms, wind and sun cause erosion, with the result that, according to geomorphologists, the coastline has receded 150 metres during the past 190 years – 80 centimetres per year. Vegetation and human activity also influence the break-up of the coastline.

Wolinski is the largest island within Poland's national frontiers. There are exceptionally beautiful landscapes with hills, picturesque sand dunes and steep cliffs. The national park covers nearly 11,000 hectares, including woodland (41 per cent), the Baltic Sea (25 per cent) and the Bay of Szczecin (18 per cent). The best-preserved woods are under strict protection (54 per cent of the area). The woods consist of 68 per cent pine; beech and oak account for 23 per cent and 7 per cent respectively. This is the first Polish sea park covered with beech wood. The beech woods are very well preserved, the structure being very similar to that of the primeval forest. The best-preserved beech woods are in two nature reserves south of Wolinski and one in the north. Wild orchids grow in the park. The plants thrive on the cliffs' soil, which is formed by the wind spreading minerals in the woods. There are nine species. The conifer woods along the coast form another exceptional family of plants. The dunes are very thinly planted. There, among other things, you will find the blue sea thistle, extremely suitable for the hard life in the dunes. In total there are 13,000 varieties of plants in the park.

Among the island's insects the one that catches the eye is the stag beetle, Poland's largest beetle. Ornithologists have counted about 230 bird species, among them the majestic sea eagle, with a wing span of up to 2.5 metres. This species is strictly protected, as the population has slumped in the last few years; only one out of each two or three couples that nest in the park every year has young. Other birds of prey are the red kite, the sparrowhawk, the hawk and the buzzard. The island also offers an ideal habitat for water birds – such as many species of gull, cormorant, mute swan, tern, grebe – and for duck species, among them the shelduck. During their migrations thousands of geese live in the park, mainly around the lakes in the eastern part. One recent project is the reintroduction of the eagle owl. The park is known for its bison reserve, too. You will also meet roe deer and wild boar. In the sea there are rare animal species, such as the grey seal and the porpoise.

◄ The sea erodes the sandy cliffs. Meanwhile the woods produce trees, but sooner or later these will drop like fallen soldiers.

▲ The apparently peaceful Baltic coast.

▼ Some trees slide down still standing upright. They die on the beach and are swallowed by the waves.

▼▼ A flight of migrating cranes. There is a fixed hierarchy in the group.

KARPATY –
PRIMEVAL BEECH FOREST

FREE AS A BIRD

In the evening candlelight appears round the village churchyard, a magic rectangle of light outlined in the dark night. My hotel smells of departed Soviet glory. I pull the curtain and an alarm goes off. It turns out to be a startled bat. Dracula is alive in the Carpathians. The night dances away on the never-abating rhythm of Boney M's *Belfast*.

The next morning I climb Mount Tarnica (1,346 metres), accompanied by a guide. From the top I look out over the Ukraine. Some heather grows on these peaks, the last remnants of vegetation. In the distance a nutcracker can be heard, but it is determined not to be seen. Otherwise there are a few tracks, nothing tangible. Not a single bird . . . What is happening here? I expect there is a true 'wilderness' across the frontier, in the Ukraine.

We follow the tracks of bison for two days. The droppings are still warm, the animals are near by, but they don't show themselves. We walk through extensive beech woods. Polish rangers suggest that we should shoot a deer in order to attract wolves or bears. 'Absolutely not!,' I say, incensed. I am in the shadowy territory bordering the Ukraine where frontier guards hunt frontier-runners and shots echo regularly, which occasionally mean that a bison is the victim. This does not detract in any way from the beauty of the forest, which glories in brilliant yellow, red and gold autumn colours.

A tree trunk has been skilfully hollowed out and now serves as sleeping quarters for a bear. The bear has left very deep tracks. A ranger tells me how he 'caught' a bear in the act of killing a wild boar. The bear hid his prey underneath branches and twigs to protect it from the wolves. Later he returned to enjoy the meat when it had become 'tenderized'. 'A bear can move a wild boar or a cow without any effort over hundreds of metres,' the ranger tells me. The farmers take precautions. They entrust their goats to large, white sheepdogs. Is this fear of bears and wolves justified? I am told the wolves are degenerating: they are lighter and weaker than they used to be – as a result of inbreeding, perhaps. There is altogether too much hunting in these woods; even the guide hunts in his leisure hours. Suddenly I spot a herd of deer in the distance. Automatically I adopt the golden rule of observation: walk against the wind when approaching animals. But my efforts produce few results. The pressure on the game is too great. The Carpathians make you dream. There are bears, wolves and bison in the woods, but you don't get to see them, because there is too much shooting going on. I meet up with some charcoal burners, though, who live in and from the woods – in the year 2008. Is this really Europe?

Bieszczady

Bieszczady is an abandoned region. After the Second World War the inhabitants were deported by the authorities of the time. The Bieszczady National Park, set up in 1973, was meanwhile extended to 27,064 hectares. Most of this area (64 per cent) is covered by woodland. The park includes parts of the Bieszczady mountains, the western outcrops of the Beskidy range, with Mount Tarnica (1,346 metres) as its highest point. The park lies in the south-eastern part of Poland and is now listed as a world biosphere reserve. Just above the woods in the foothills – beech and spruce – is the so-called poloniny or mountain pasture. The treeless tops of the mountains, surrounded by green woods, make up a unique area of natural beauty which has hardly been influenced by man. It is an oasis of quiet, healthy air and crystal-clear water.

In the park the beech dominates (85 per cent). Together with the maple and the spruce, it makes up the typical vegetation of the Carpathians, to be seen on the mountain slopes and in the valleys. The beech forest grows up to an altitude of 1,150 metres, bordering on the mountain pastures, interrupted by blue and red bilberries, grass, alders and rowan trees. There is no sub-alpine brushwood in Biesczady. The vegetation is very rich, with about 900 species of vascular plants, of which 42 are protected species. Several plants are typical for the eastern Carpathians, among them mosses, lichens and fungi. Sedge and wood fescue overgrow the depressions of the dry mountain flanks. Bieszczady has 200 rare animal species, among them the European bison, which was introduced in 1963, the brown bear, the lynx, the wildcat, the wolf, deer and the wild boar. There are more than 100 species of bird, among them the Ural owl, the dunnock, the red-throated pipit and the imperial eagle. Among the reptiles the adder is noticeably present.

ISLAND

SKAFTAFELL

LABORATORY OF LIFE

A park in the shadow of a glacier as big as Corsica, with two glacier tongues, including the enormous Vatnajökull. These sheets of ice were formed over millions of years. In the lagoon there are blocks of ice 30 metres high. Scores of these are shifting towards the sea. A loud crack shatters the silence. From time to time there is the sound of an explosion – another one breaking loose and falling into the water. I never knew that ice had so many colours when the glaciers mingle with the sea. Farther on is the peninsula with its towering cliffs. Seventy species of birds live here, of which a large number are migratory. I feel as though I am walking through the set of Hitchcock's *The Birds*. On the ground is a carpet of lichen and shrubs which have trouble keeping upright, lashed by the never-abating wind. It seems like the cradle of the world.

For half an hour I am threatened by a skua. These predatory gulls, as large as a buzzard, rise high and then dive down like an arrow. Terns are breeding in a field of moss. I could watch the colonies for ever.

The climb to the top of the glacier is hard. The peaks soon disappear in the clouds and for a moment I feel as if I am on the moon. I see glimpses of the Scottish Highlands in these peaks, but they are rougher and very volcanic. There is a deafening silence. In the mud there are tracks of swans. The wind moves the feathers of the birds in the opposite direction. Fields of birds stand planted in the black sand, like a sea of feathers. The real sea is 15 kilometres away. The meltwater from the glacier runs towards it. Because I lack suitable equipment I have to give up the climb (up to 2,000 metres).

Puffins look as if they are anchored to the ground: live black candles that allow you to come up to within 80 centimetres of them. Skuas attack the puffins. The iron laws of life and death apply here. I witness the whole life cycle of the birds on the black sand, from egg to adult animal. A fulmar's egg hatches. The chick flounders on its back and waves its feet high as it tries to break the eggshell. A few ravens – super-predators – circle among the gulls, looking for lost chicks. When I approach a fulmar on the cliffs, it spits in my direction to frighten me off. The puffins look after their young. Not surprisingly, they have only one each year. To be faced with the cycle of life and death, with one bird in the role of predator and the other prey, is an awesome experience. At the bottom of the cliffs I can see a group of seals. Four otters walk along tidily in line. A heron keeps an eye on them.

Skaftafell

The Vatnajökull National Park, set up in 2008, covers Skaftafell, Jokulsargljufur, the major part of the Vatnajökull glacier, the Hagonguhraun, Veidivatnahraun and the lava fields of Vesturoraefi, the Snaefell mountain, Eyjabakkar and a part of Hraun north of the glacier. It is the largest park in Europe (12,000 km^2, almost 12 per cent of the surface area of Iceland). The Langisjor zone may well later become part of the park too. Skaftafell contains a number of nature's jewels. The rugged landscape, the mountains, flora and fauna leave a lasting impression. There are no roads in the park, but there is a network of paths.

▲ *Untouched oceans of space – an ideal place for introspection.*

▶ *A predatory gull. Whoever dares enter its territory is immediately beleaguered.*

▶ *In scenes like this the inquisitive faces of seals frequently pop up.*

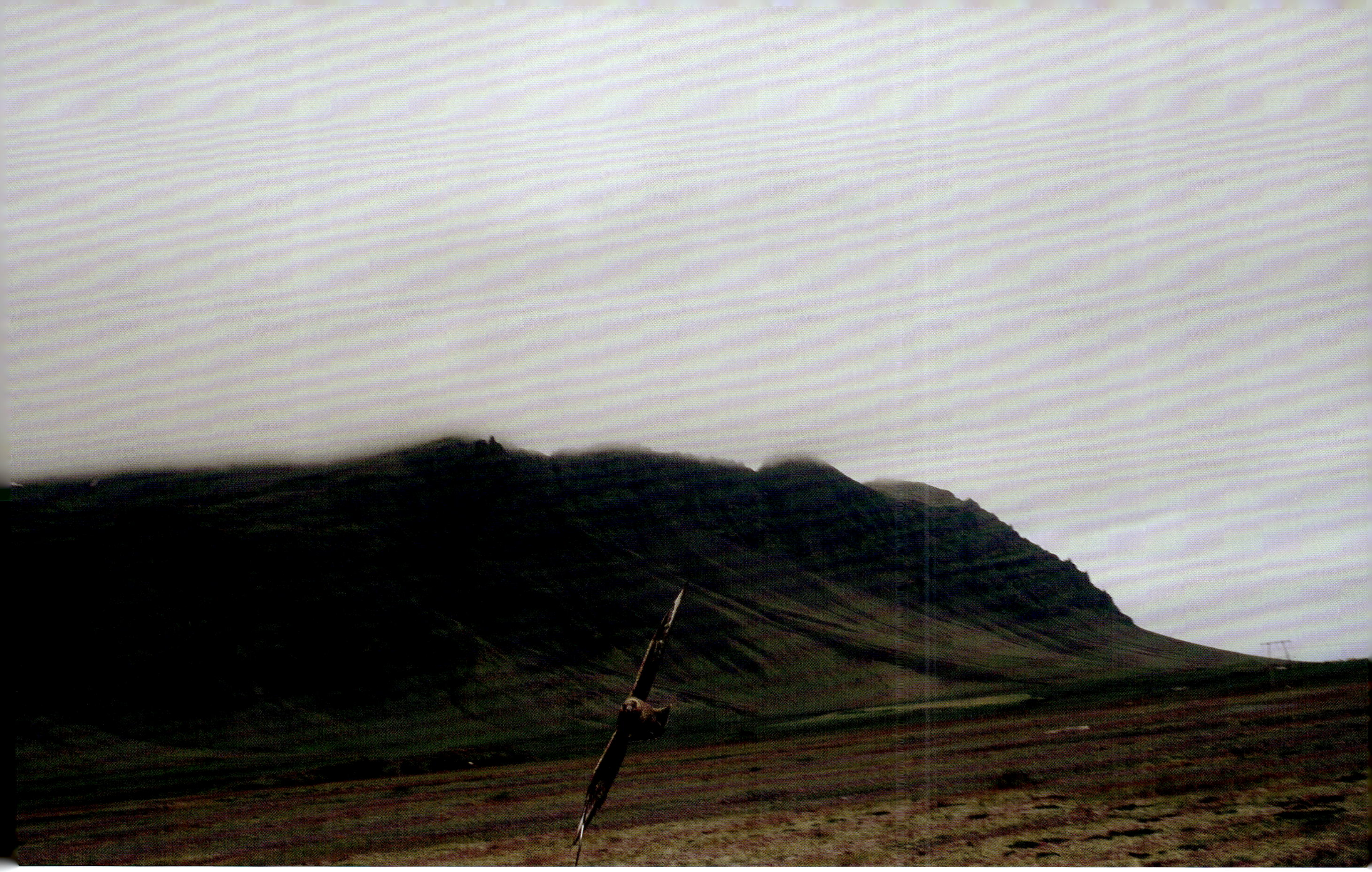

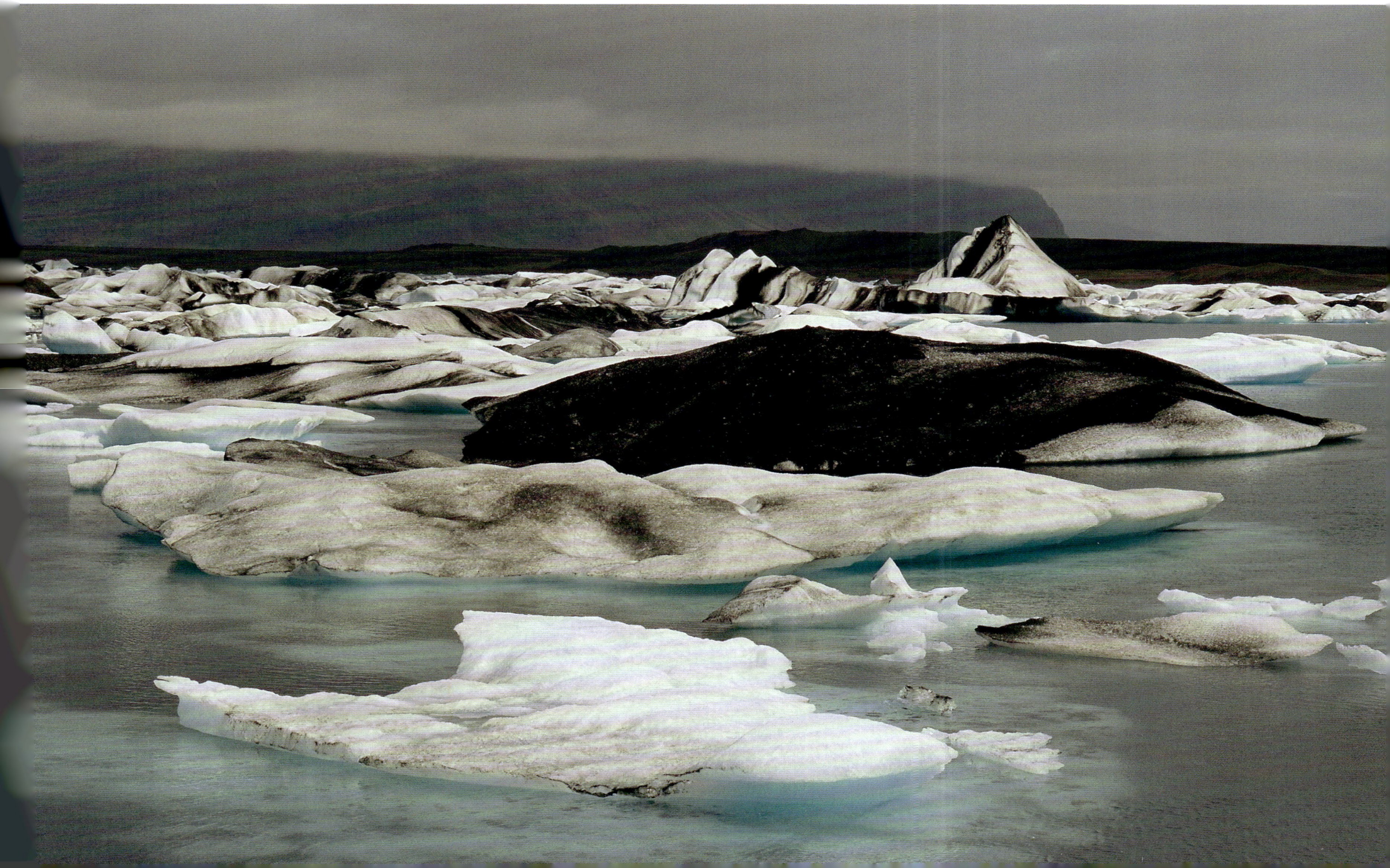

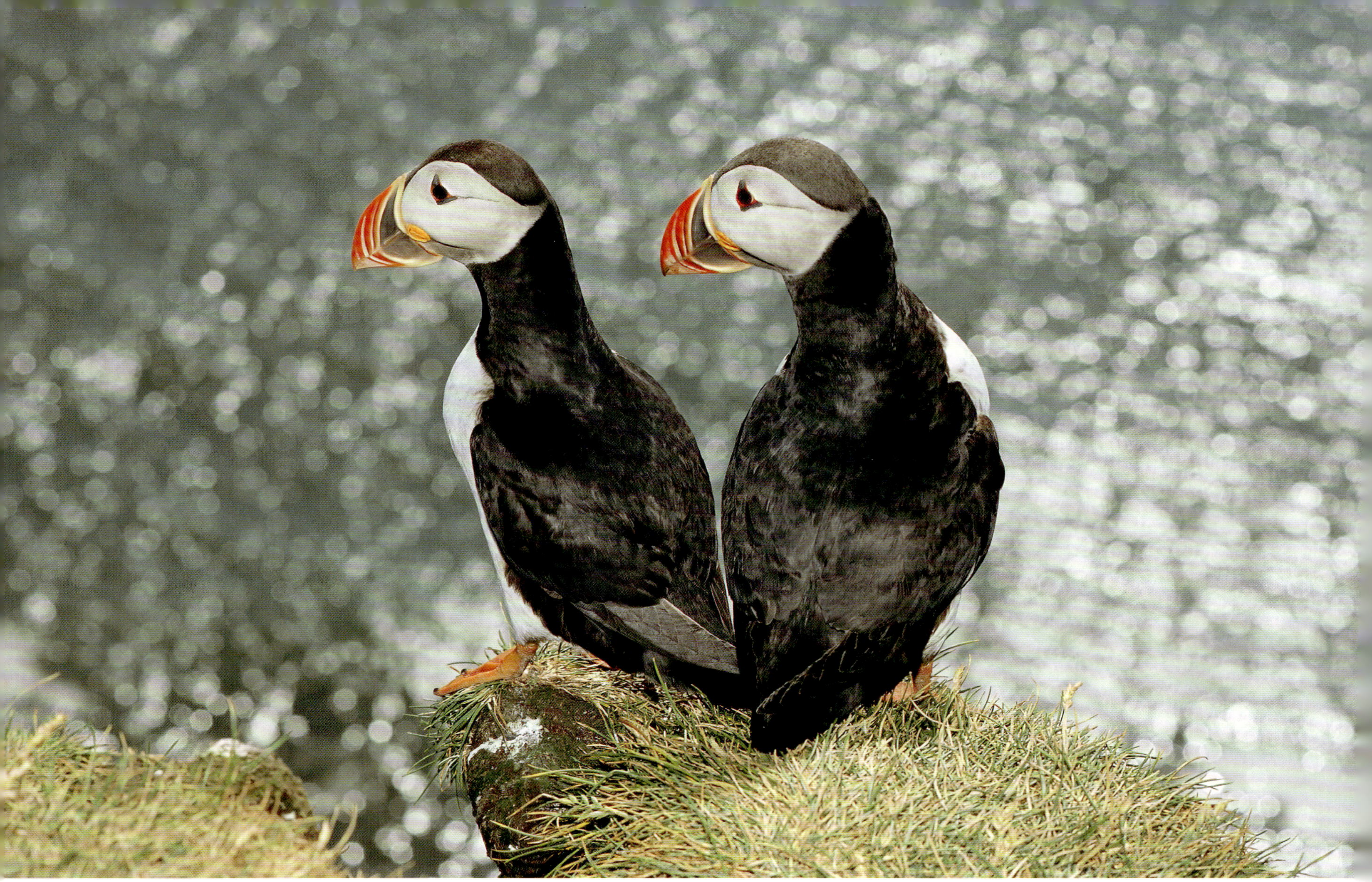

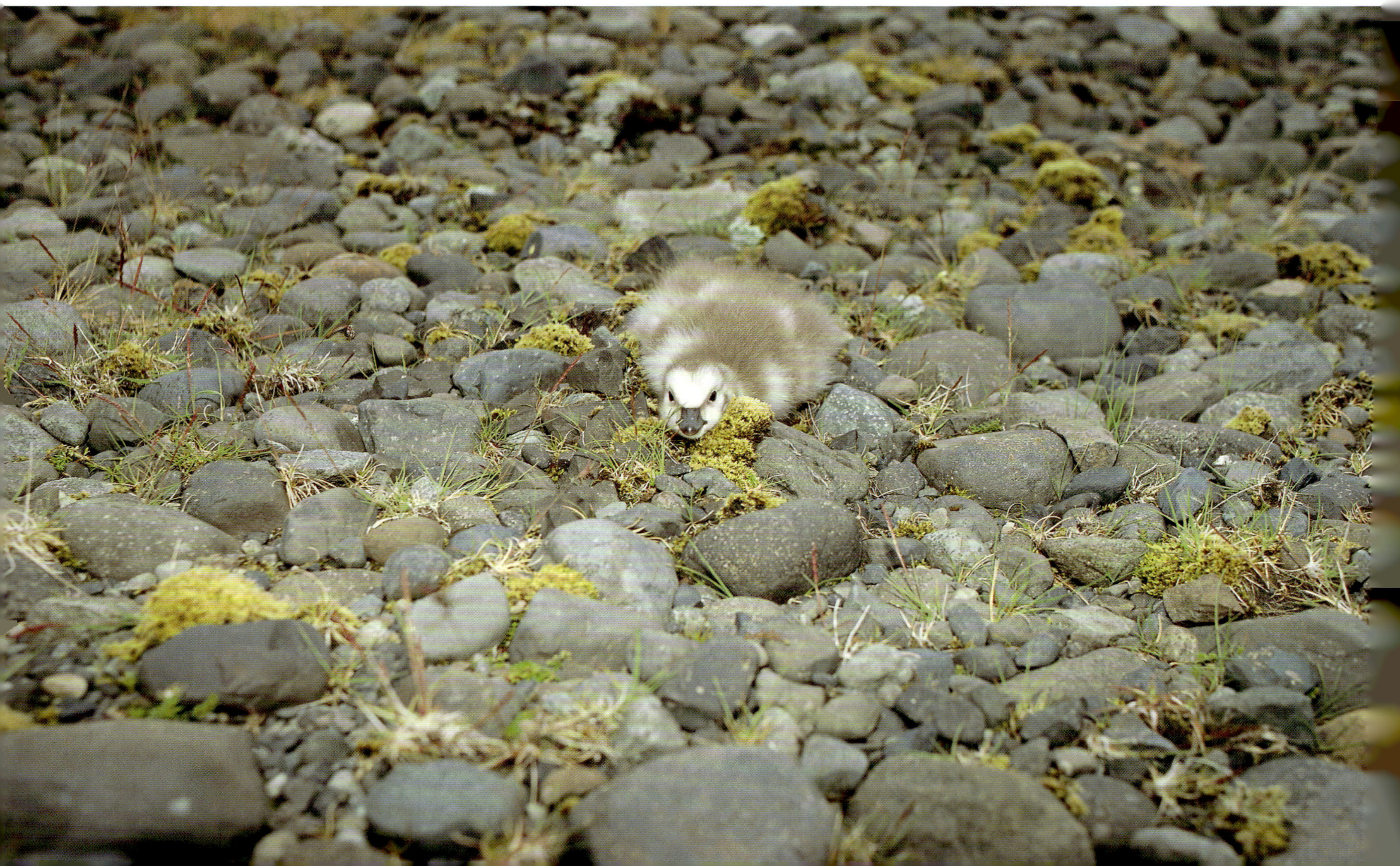

◄ Puffins are air acrobats and very social birds. They are continually menaced by the aggressive predatory gulls.

▲ A glacier tongue in all its icy splendour. Difficult to walk on, but fascinating!

▼ Volcanic sandy beaches where birds continually search the environment.

◄ A gosling has accidentally become separated from the flock. Instinctively it lies flat on its belly so that it will be less visible (behaviour known as mimetism).

▼▼ Blocks of ice as large as a building break loose from the glacier tongue.

NORGE

LOFOTEN – LAPLAND

LOFOTEN – ARCHIPELAGO AND ARCTIC COAST

MOUNTAINS RISING FROM THE SEA

I am in the Lofoten islands in northern Norway, going to look for orcas. In late autumn the orcas come into the fjords, following the herrings, which spend the winter in the cold water of the fjords. The animals live on a diet of herrings, an adult orca swallowing up to 70 kilograms of fish a day. Every year the spectacle of the orcas attracts tourists and scientists, who gaze for hours at the waves in the hope of seeing a tail or dorsal fin. I am in Svolvaer, the 'capital' of the Lofoten, where the orca season starts at the beginning of winter, although this year the fish have kept us waiting, as the water has been too warm and the herrings have delayed entering the fjords.

The wind determines when we will set out to sea. The dark water of the fjords contrasts sharply with the cliffs covered in snow and ice. This is the mythical high north above the Arctic Circle. We sail out on a wild sea. In the distance dorsal fins emerge from the water. Visibility is limited. It's like looking for the proverbial needle in a haystack, in this case the enormous mass of water of the fjords. A mud bank shows itself. This usually means that there are no orcas in the immediate vicinity. The scene is altogether sublime. The light drops slowly away, the white tops of the snowy mountains contrasting with the endless, black sea. There has been no trace of orcas for the last couple of days. It is beginning to get quite dark. In winter it is practically night by around four o'clock in the afternoon.

A fisherman is throwing fish offal into the water. Above our heads seagulls and sea eagles circle; they will lose no time in recovering the fish. Soon a whirling dance of wings develops. Suddenly a dorsal fin slices through the water. Then a ballet starts with two males – recognizable by their large, upright fins – in the principal role. The females soon come very briefly out of the water to look at us. Two or three times I find myself being stared at by an orca that has risen high out of the water, its white belly turned towards us. It is a moment of sheer beauty. The dorsal fins can be as much as 1½ metres high, in symmetry with the surrounding mountains that rise out of the sea. I register the size of the animals: they are up to 8 metres long.

When the orcas feel themselves 'caught out' during the hunt – with all those little boats around them it looks like a safari – they slap their tails hard on the water. From time to time one dashes underneath the boat, and I see its silhouette flash in the water. Suddenly the orcas gather together and surround a school of herrings. The dorsal fins of the males look like tightly stretched

sails. The size and the power of these predators continues to impress. What from a distance looks like a buoy turns out to be an orca, briefly diving out of the water with a third of its body. Just a flash, three seconds at the most. Why?

Lofoten

The Lofoten form an archipelago (1,227 km²) about 200 kilometres above the Arctic Circle. There are about 170 kilometres between Fiskebøl, the most northerly island, and Å in the south. Thanks to the warm Gulf Stream the climate here is much milder than in other regions lying at the same latitude, such as Alaska and Greenland. The winters are mild and the summers relatively cool.

INTERVIEW WITH CONSERVATIONIST HEIKKE VESTER, OF OCEAN SOUNDS

How do you explain the presence of orcas in the fjords in winter?
They follow the herring throughout the year and during the winter the fish approach the Norwegian coast. But the migration pattern has changed and nowadays the herring do not come into the Vestfjord any more as they used to. Last winter there were hardly any orcas in Vestfjord and Tysfjord. The herring now pass the winter more in the north and deeper in the sea. No one knows why. How will the fish population evolve in the years to come? It's a good question. Could this change be a result of global warming?

Exactly how many orcas are there in the Lofoten?
The exact number of orcas is not known. There has been mention of 1,500 to 2,000 animals in the northern Atlantic Ocean, but these numbers have not been confirmed.

What are the main threats to them?
Fishnets in which the orcas get caught, overfishing, environmental pollution (oil, PCBs, etc.), the noise of ships and sonar.

◄ *The boundless peace of the fjords. Even here, though, the fish stock is shrinking.*

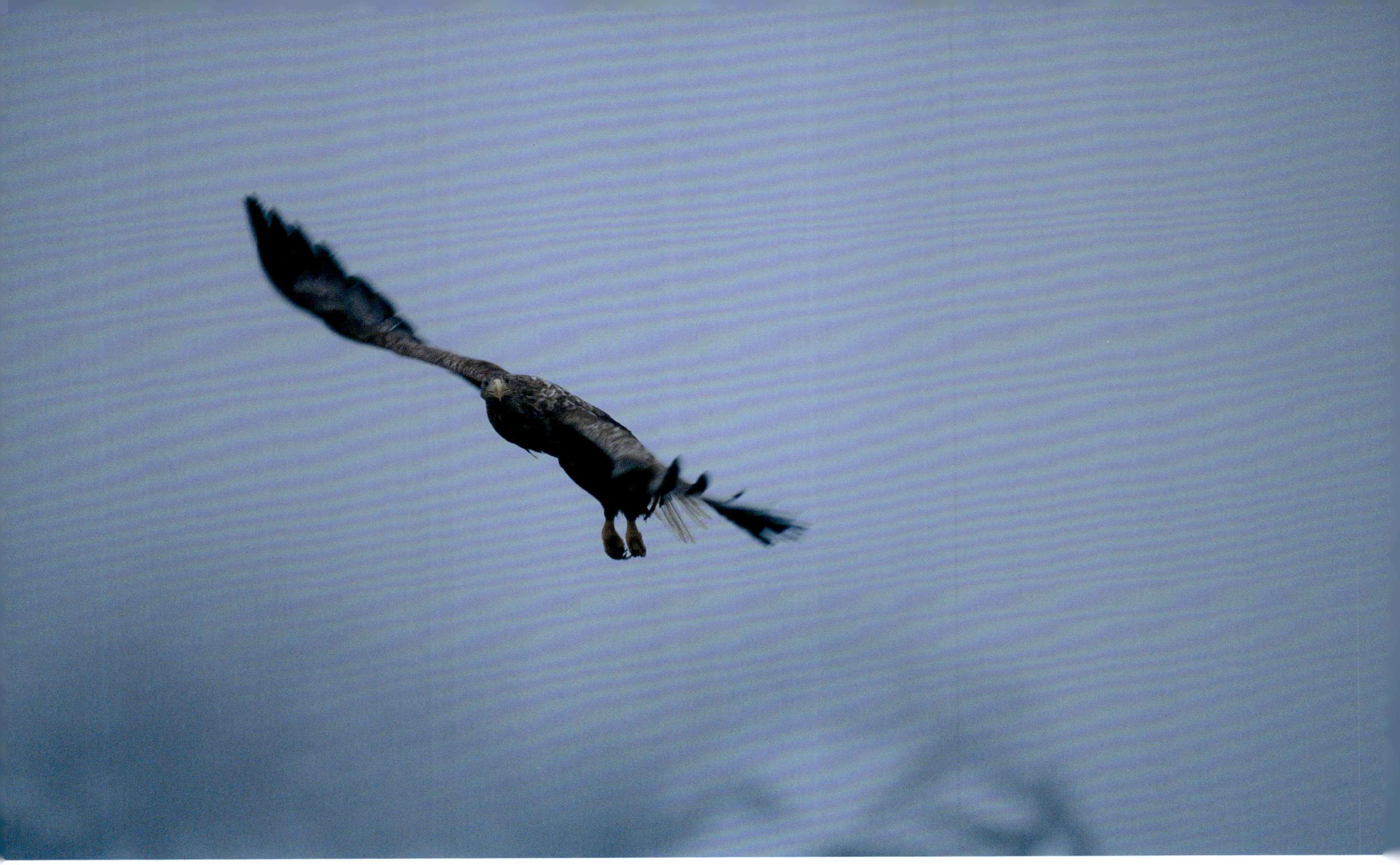

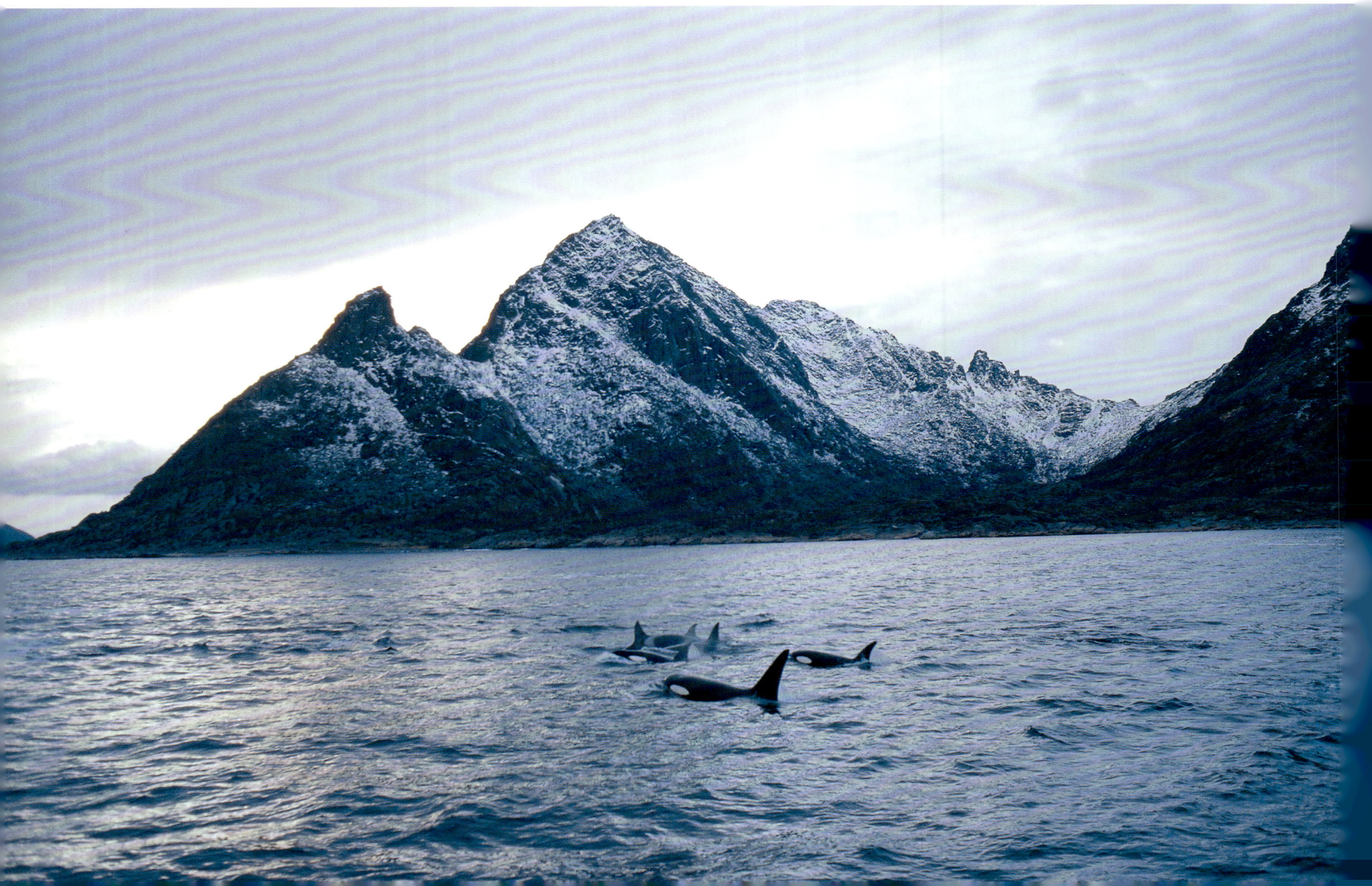

The orca is the largest of the dolphin family. It lives in the cold seas of Patagonia, Canada, the United States, Alaska, Greenland, Iceland and Norway. In Norway 40 pods have been recorded, each time with 8 to 25 animals. Local scientists have identified 550 different individuals. They photograph the dorsal fin and the visible part of their back when the animals come to the surface, and from the shape of the fin, the marks and scars, etc., they can recognize each animal. The fin is their 'fingerprint'. On males the dorsal fin is up to 1,5 metre high. The fascination of these beasts is timeless. In the Lofoten drawings have been found dating from the end of the Ice Age. You can recognize the form of the animal, life size, more than 7 metres long.

A pod of orcas is led by the eldest female. The animals stay in the same group for their whole life. Orcas 'speak' different dialects, which makes it possible for them to recognize their own group easily. They send out a signal from their frontal brains. That sound is reflected back to the brain by echolocation via the lower jaw. In this way they can get a 'sound picture' of schools of herring, boats, related species or whatever obstacle they meet. The sound carries as far as 20 kilometres.

Orcas are not easy to observe, not least because they spend 99 per cent of their time under water. They hunt mainly in the night, when the herring come to the surface. They surround the school and chase them upwards in so-called carousel feeding. Then they hit them with their tails and then eat the stunned or dead herring.

◄   The majestic white-tailed sea eagle lets itself float in the wind. The lack of fish compels him – highly unusually – to beg for food.

◄   The dorsal fin of a male orca is as big as a man. I stood eye to eye with this mammal, an experience I shall remember all my life.

▲   Birds follow the orcas. Wherever they are swimming, the remains of their prey will surface. Even the majestic sea eagle is part of the procession.

▼   According to old tales, the sea eagle used to be more widely distributed.

LAPLAND – TUNDRA

GIANT CRABS AND SEAS OF LICHEN

I am approaching Jarfjord near Kirkenes on the Russian frontier. 'Actually, this is a scientific experiment that got out of hand,' explains the guide, as we step on board his Zodiac. 'In 1961 Russian scientists took seven king crabs from Kamchatka in the Pacific to Murmansk, 300 kilometres from here. Ten years later the fishermen caught the first king crabs in their nets. Since then the crabs have become a plague. They have adapted perfectly and now they colonize the fjords. They are moving towards the south.' Anton, a Russian, dives into the ice-cold water. For several minutes we only see air bubbles coming up. When he comes up again he has two crabs in his hand. A little farther on floats a buoy. Anton and Lars pull up the crab basket. It is full to bursting. We travel back across the calm fjord. 'Did you know that these crabs reproduce fantastically fast?' asks the guide. 'An adult crab has up to half a million eggs. Assuming that 2 per cent of them survive, each crab has 10,000 offspring!'

I drive through an impressive, empty country that adds new meaning to the concept of 'extensive'. Suddenly a herd of 'wild' reindeer runs across the road. In fact the animals belong to the Sami herdsmen, who keep them for their meat and their hide. Outside, the shrill shriek of a buzzard shatters the silence; a raven croaks past. We are looking for lemmings, which are a feast for predators and birds of prey. Alas, we don't get to see any during our drive of 240 kilometres through a patchwork of lichen and stone, with the blue sea as background. I want to see the gyrfalcon, which feeds on lemmings. In the end I have to be satisfied with a stuffed one, recently knocked down on one of the few roads in this vast country.

Norwegian Lapland

At the level of the North Cape – the most northerly point of Europe – Norway is a 'moon landscape' of tundra, rocks and water. Around Kirkenes birches grow; farther north you no longer see trees. Kirkenes (9,500 inhabitants) is Norway's most northerly town, on the Russian border, more than 2,300 kilometres north of Oslo. The little town lies in the thinly populated Finmark (72,000 inhabitants, surface area 48,637 km²). This 'Norwegian Lapland' is an extensive tundra area, situated 500 kilometres above the Arctic Circle.

Crab or crayfish?

The red king crab, also called the giant crab or the Kamchatka crab (Paralithodes), is not a true crab: it is related to the hermit crab and belongs to the Anomura. This species is, like the Chinese mitten crab, an exotic species which occurs in places where it does not belong and eats the food of other species. From an ecological point of view the king crab is more disastrous than the Chinese mitten crab. Originally it occurred only in Alaska and Kamchatka, but now it has reached the northern North Sea via Norway (where it was introduced).

Nice but harmful

The king crab is a delicacy. The snow-white meat is considered a real treat, for which the price can go up to nearly 80 euros per kilo. But there is a reverse side to the culinary medal: king crabs cause great damage on the ocean floor. Norway has strictly tightened their catch quota. Environmental associations have even argued for the complete extermination of the crabs – except in their original habitat – to prevent further damage. It is not surprising that the king crab does so well above the Arctic Circle. It has hardly any natural enemies there. Only the wolf fish, cod and some seabirds can deal with small to medium-sized king crabs.

▶ *The mythical North Cape, where in summer the sun never sets. The fauna and flora take full advantage of this period.*

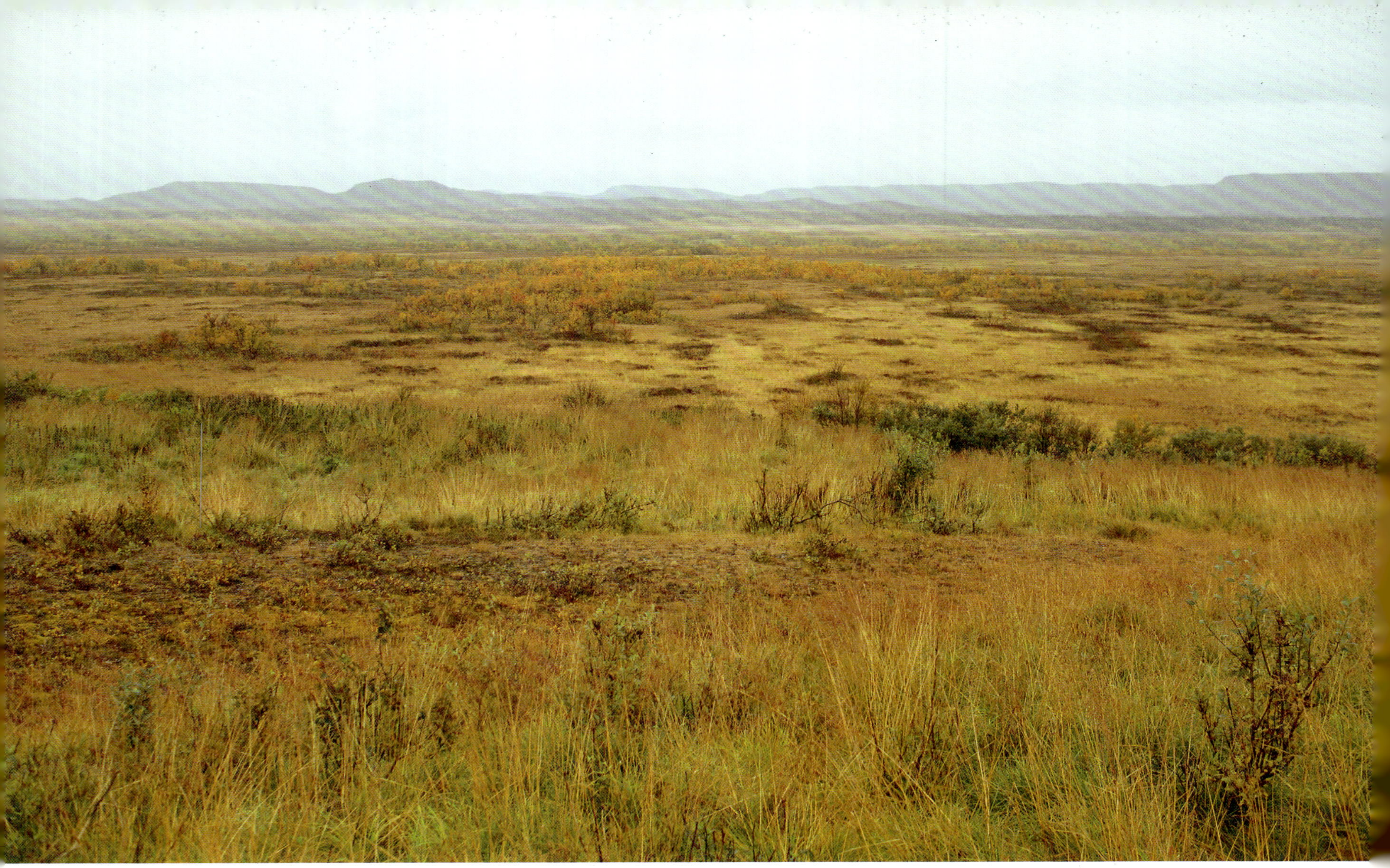

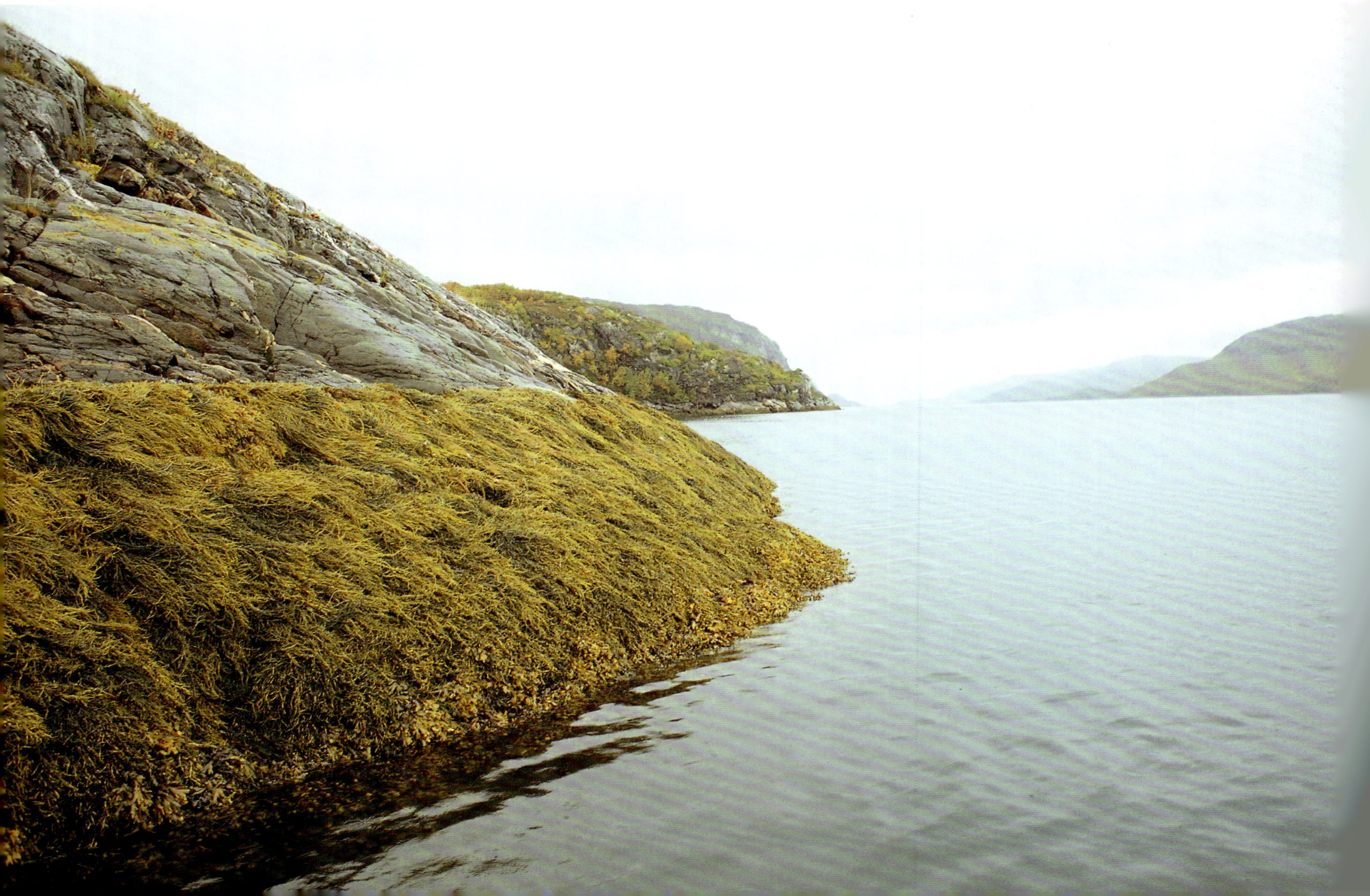

◄ Extensive plains dotted with dwarf trees. They grow at most a few centimetres every 100 years.

◄ Not far from Murmansk, fighter aircraft and warships from the Second World War rest at the bottom of the sea.

▼ Stalin's king crabs were imported from Kamchatka to Murmansk. Now they flourish in abundance, eat the sea bed empty and colonize the fjords in the north of Norway.

▶ Herring gulls and seagulls in the water. On the sea bed below there is an army of king crabs.

▼ The snowy owl. This heavenly creature is a nocturnal predator, which adapts itself to the midnight sun in the summer.

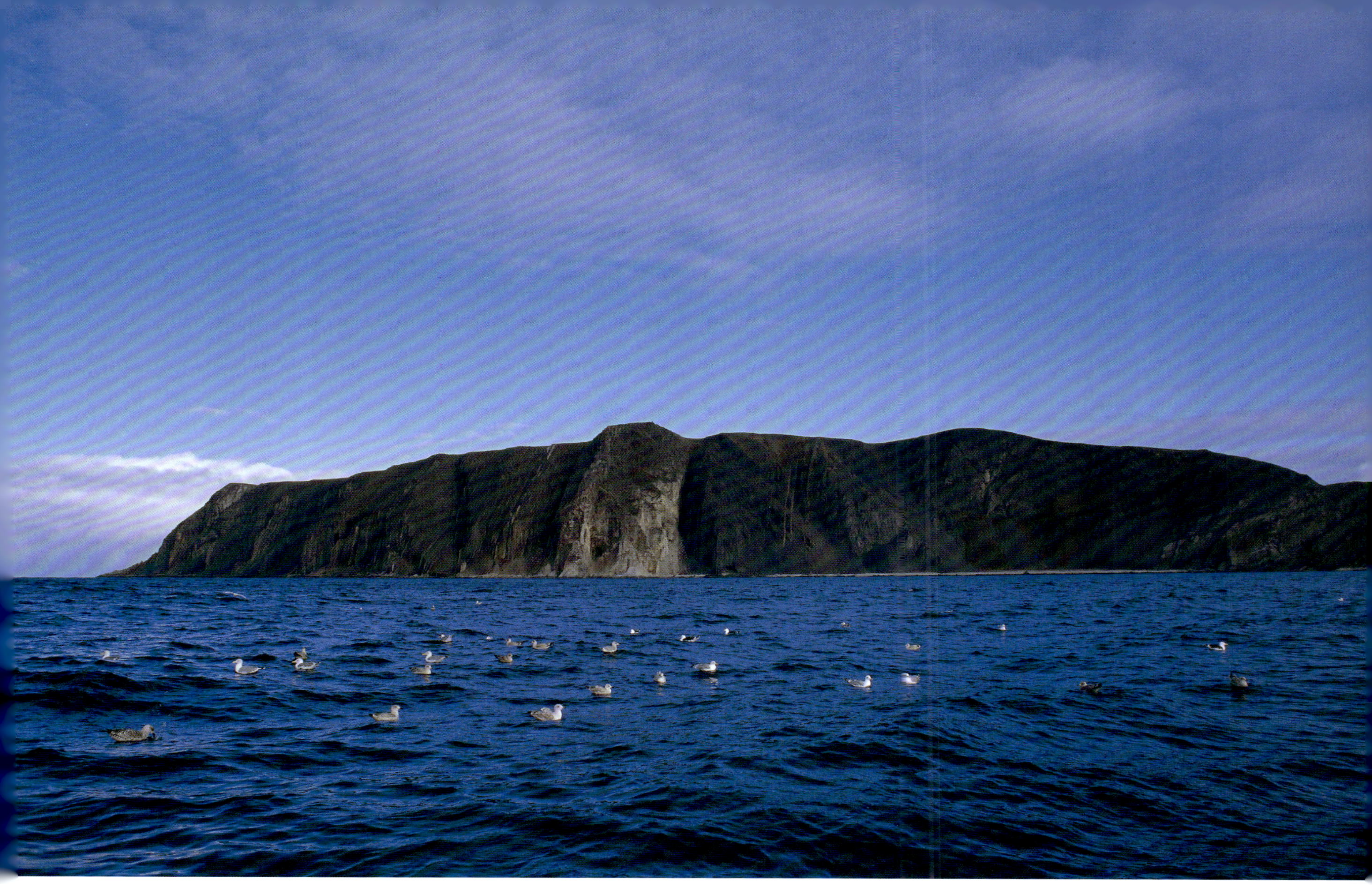
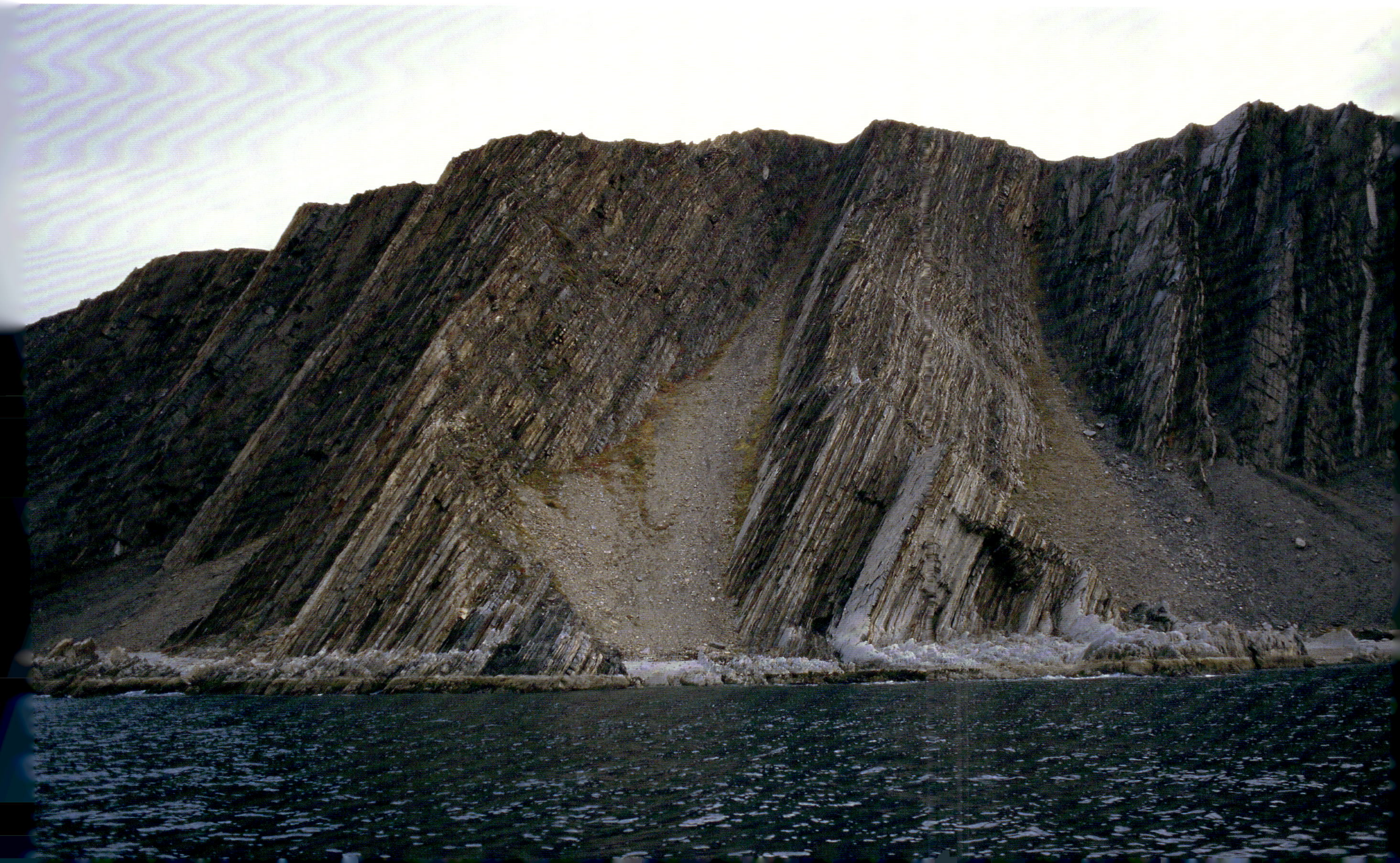

SCOTLAND

HIGHLANDS

LAND OF EMPTINESS AND LOCHS

On the deep indented west coast of Scotland there are lochs, glens, hillsides overgrown with heather, islands lashed by the wind, limitless sandy beaches and cliffs like lonely watchmen high above waves agitated by a storm. This is a land of extremes. I am transported back to primitive times, lost in a sea of space, with Ben Nevis (1.367 metres) the only beacon. Everything is bathed in silence and breathes mystery.

After continuous rain, the burns – gentle streams or shallow, fast-flowing rivulets – can swell into powerful streams. Sometimes I feel as though I am walking through a box of bricks that has been turned upside down: all the stones are higgledy-piggledy and jumbled up. The stones of the scree are rather smaller than those in the brick field, and wet and slippery in the rain; the moss does not make walking on it any easier. However, the large amount of water that gushes on the oldest mountains in Europe does fine things to the landscape. The rocks hold no water, with the result that everywhere burns, streams and waterfalls form. Over thousands of years ponds have been filled up with sphagnum moss, the basis for the moorland that feeds sheep, deer and game birds.

On the Atlantic coast I see a seal, a couple of puffins, a flight of petrels and terns. Seabirds and seals feel they are safe near the inaccessible cliffs. Deep red anemones and bright yellow lichens contrast with the bright blue sea. The cliffs have an irresistibly dramatic air because of their steep and inaccessible character, and the strength of the waves that batter them. I hear the sea crashing, soft against hard. Chunks of broken rock pile up off the coast or are carried out deeper into the sea. They are treacherous for ships.

The Highlands

Through the middle of the Scottish Highlands runs the Great Glen, a valley that was carved out by glaciers in the Ice Age. The mountains and the lakes along this valley, which include Loch Ness, were formed millions of years ago. Here, near Fort William, Ben Nevis rules. The largest part of the Highlands lies above 900 metres and consists mainly of desolate expanses of peat and heather. In addition long stretches of valleys alternate with deep lochs and harsh granite peaks. The massive mountains tell of prehistory, 440 million years ago, when two tectonic plates bumped into each other. The resultant folds stretched from the later Newfoundland across Ireland and Scotland (the earlier Caledonia) as far as Greece. The Highlands were severely split by erosion. After the Caledonian folds followed the Hercynian (300 million years ago) and the Alpine folds (65 million years ago). The shifts in the Earth's crust brought about gigantic fractures that were the source of great rock formations, spread about like armour plating. Scotland lies a lot farther north than the Alps. The winters are fierce and no trees grow above 700 metres. Snow lies on the top of Ben Nevis all through the summer. It can be winter on the highest peaks until well into May. The Highlands have a reputation to keep up.

WILDCAT

The wildcat is the iconic symbol of 'wild' Scotland. But the hazardous position in which the wildcat now finds itself illustrates the difference between myth and reality. Just as Scotland itself is considered to be 'wild', but the current landscape is in fact the result of human activities, so the wildcat has almost vanished because of interbreeding with the domestic cat, which man introduced. The wildcat is also a victim of grouse shooting, whether deliberate or not. What does the future hold? Because of interbreeding with the house cat it is difficult to decide exactly what is a wildcat and how many wildcats there are in Scotland. Regular hunting is a pernicious thought, as is the confrontation of the house cat with the wildcat on its terrain. A ban on cat-hunting is a possible solution. In addition, the owners of pets should be encouraged to have their animals neutered in areas where the wildcat is encountered, according to the John Muir Trust.

INTERVIEW WITH CONSERVATIONIST MIKE DANIELS, OF THE JOHN MUIR TRUST

What makes the ecosystem of the Highlands so unique?
People relish the 'wilderness' aspect, with low population density and wide open spaces without trees. But make no mistake: the Highlands are the result not of a natural process but of thousands of years of deforestation and depopulation. In addition the area has for centuries been overgrazed by sheep and deer, and all large predators (lynx, bear, wolf), and a number of mammals (beaver, aurochs) and birds (sea eagle, osprey, red kite) have died out. Overgrazing and climate change encouraged the formation of peat. Now the Highlands form a barren, windswept, treeless expanse. Spectacular, but certainly not natural or original! On the positive side you can find high mountains here with an alpine character (above 900 metres). This is the only real wilderness, together with some cliffs and the coastline. On the other hand there is no natural tree line and very little woodland (Scotland is the least forested country in Europe). Because of the barren landscape the hundreds of mountains are even more noticeable. After a few hours' walking you exchange the sea for high mountains. There are also hundreds of magnificent islands and miles of beaches.

In what way are the Highlands wild?
There is a 'wilderness', but – as I've explained – it is neither natural nor pristine. Every square foot is used by man for sheep or deer, which are hunted, and for walking or climbing. A feeling of space is easy to find in Scotland. The Highlands are miles from anywhere, and you experience the elements and nature there. The John Muir Trust, for which I work, appeals to those positive feelings. We want to protect 'wild' zones, to reverse the trend and give nature a second chance.

What is the position on biodiversity?
Despite the absence of the original large mammals there is great biodiversity. There is just as much rain in the Atlantic oak woods as there is in the tropical rainforests. You will find lichens and liverworts. On the coast there are seals and salmon, next to hundreds of thousands of gannets, puffins, guillemots and shearwaters that nest on the Scottish islands and the cliffs. There are also many otters, pine martens and black grouse. Unfortunately populations of red squirrels and capercaillies are declining. The balance is being restored, thanks to the recent reintroduction of red kites and sea eagles and the natural recolonization of the osprey; the planned reintroduction of the beaver will help too. You will come across red deer in large numbers. Peat moors are probably the most unique biotope in north Scotland. This is marshland where rare wading birds breed and specific insects and plants are found.

What message do you want to pass on to conservationists?
We devote ourselves to the conservation and protection of wild land. We want to spur people on to experience this 'wilderness' and to respect it. We want to restore the natural processes by reducing overgrazing by sheep and deer. In this way the woodland (and other habitats) will have a chance to regenerate. With regeneration insects, birds and other mammals will return. We don't just limit ourselves to the management of the zones which

The red deer and roe deer are native to Scotland; the Sika deer and fallow deer are introduced. Large herds of red deer are part of Scotland. Failing game stewardship allowed the population to grow to impossible numbers (the largest population in the world). In addition, the number of red deer has increased massively as a result of deforestation – the animals now live on treeless hills – and burning off, and because of the elimination of the wolf and the lynx. Consequently in many areas biodiversity is now under pressure. Scotland is one of the most highly deforested countries in Europe and has virtually no natural tree line. The authorities are now working towards a more sustainable stewardship of the deer population and want to compensate for the damage caused by large herds. There has also been some talk about the reintroduction of large predators to restart the process of natural selection. For more information, see www.jmt.org/home.asp.

we own or which we manage in partnership: we also want to encourage others to follow our example. Hence we are running a campaign against projects that threaten the wild land. Scotland wants to be an important player in the field of renewable energy within Europe and so engage in the battle against global warming. Unfortunately there are now plans to site wind farms on an industrial scale on the tops of dozens of hills and connect these to the national grid via huge power pylons. This will not only despoil the landscape but also threaten the biodiversity and carbon balance of very sensitive habitats. The current 'wind hype' follows years of similar short-term management, such as the planting of exotic conifers in the 1980s, excessive burning off, overgrazing by sheep and deer, quarrying and ski developments.

How can the Highlands be preserved for the future?
It isn't just about the preservation of the 'wilderness' but also about an ongoing education of the whole community. We believe that tourism and ecotourism make wide-ranging and sustainable development possible. That does not mean ambitious projects that bring in money and provide work in the short term, because some of those projects will cost money in the long term. For instance, we now use tax revenues to restore the areas that were affected by planting woods which were paid for with taxpayers' money in the first place.

What particularly appeals to you as an ecologist in the Highlands?
The feeling of wildness and the wild animals. Moreover, the area possesses every potential for sustainable management to the benefit of both the environment and people.

How do you see the future of this wonderful area?
To be honest, it could go in any direction. The planned industrial projects around renewable energy threaten a large zone of wild land. As a result of global warming the alpine-arctic climates of the high mountains are under pressure and the mountain hare and alpine red grouse are at risk. But I see the possibility of sustainable management if we recognize the intrinsic value of the 'wilderness' alongside its tourist potential. It is also important that the European agricultural policy should be adapted. Sustainable carbon management is urgent, too. Scotland's peat subsoil contains an important part of the carbon stock in Europe's subsoil. We can support ecosystems by carbon-neutral management.

▲ The yeti of the Highlands or the Loch Ness monster?

▶ In this glen I accompanied a biologist who catches wildcats and examines their DNA. Inter-breeding with house cats threatens the survival of this species.

▼ The local name for this eroded cliff is the Old Man of Hoy. The white fulmar is a lovely contrast to the blue of the ocean.

▼▼ These beehive-like cliffs are alive with birds, shrieking, flying and raiding. I saw a pod of orcas here, looking for seals.

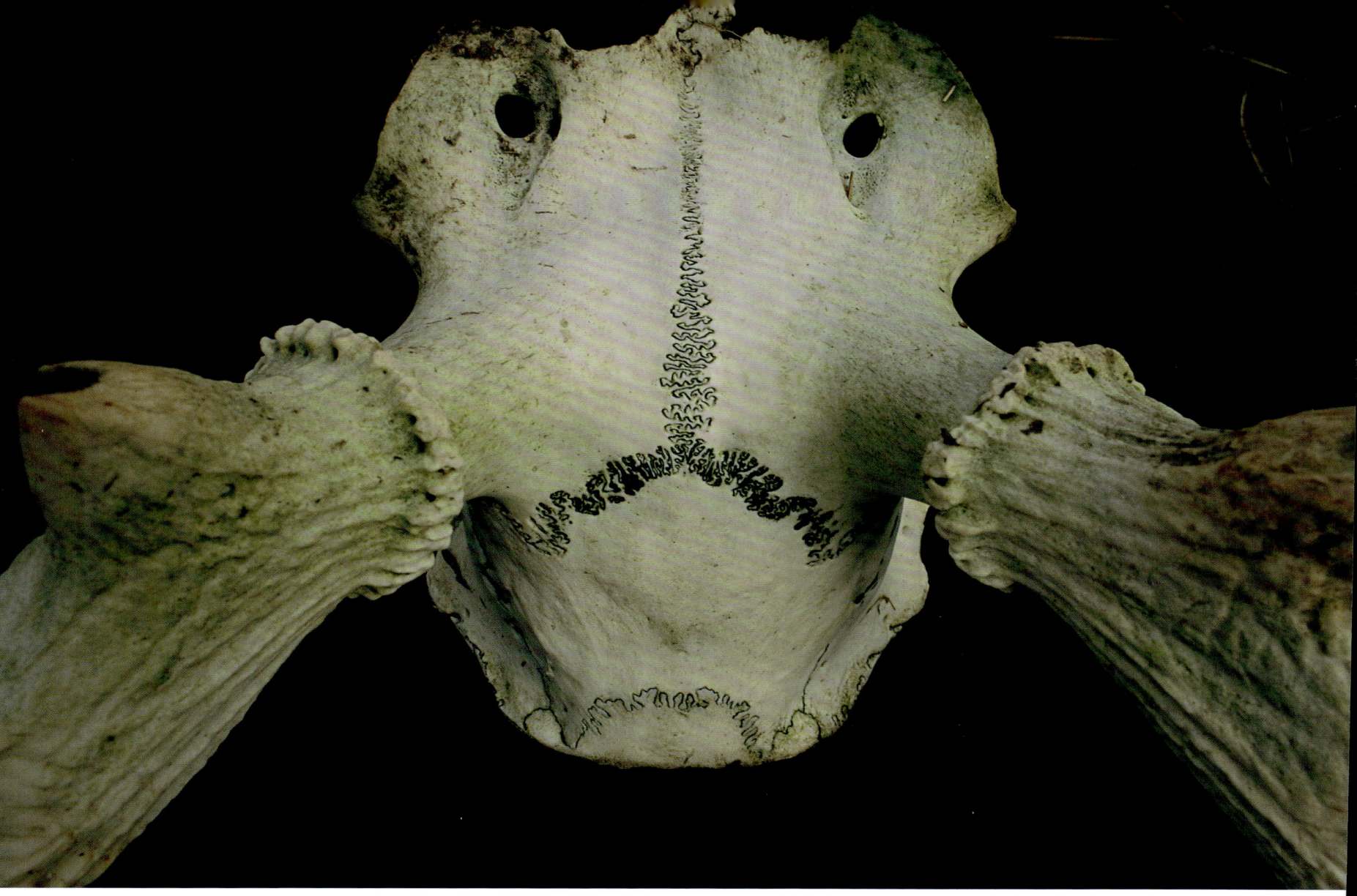

'I haven't got any special religion this morning. My God is the God of Walkers. If you walk hard enough, you probably don't need any other God.'

Bruce Chatwin, In Patagonia, 1977

▲   *The skull of a deer, like a death mask.*

▶   *In the glens the roar of the deer can be heard day and night. There are so many hinds that sometimes it looks as if a large part of the valley has started moving.*

▼   *The Arctic tern, as if frozen in flight.*

HOHE TAUERN

HOHE TAUERN – GLACIER STREAMS

WHERE ICE SINGS THE SONG OF THE WIND

Everything is white and much more impressive than I had expected. An imperial eagle circles high above me. I position myself opposite a frozen waterfall and wait for a lammergeier to arrive. In valleys that are hard to get to I move about on skis, as if on chamois leather. The surroundings are magnificent, with a thick carpet of snow. The silhouette of a raven shows up against the blue sky. There are bluish frozen waterfalls like gigantic pillars cast in wax. This is the setting in which the lammergeier is likely to be, but alas, he does not show himself today, except as a vague shadow through binoculars. I do see plenty of crows, however. But after half an hour the weather deteriorates. A storm is brewing. I can't see my hand in front of my eyes. Everything turns white and the wind whistles around my ears . . .

Ice Age

Hohe Tauern is a land of glaciers. Glaciers form in places where summer temperatures are not high enough to melt the snow that fell in the winter. Year after year layers of snow pile up and gradually, under increasing pressure, these become ice. A glacier is not a rigid body but flows slowly towards the valley as a mass. During its descent great cracks form in the ice. Although the Alpine glaciers have been shrinking for many years, there is an impressive number of mountain glaciers in Hohe Tauern. Think of the Pasterzen glacier, 9 kilometres long and 19 km² in size, or the massif of the Großvenediger, protected by the ice of the largest continuous glacier surfaces of the eastern Alps.

After fire, ice gave shape to Hohe Tauern. During the Ice Age the Alpine glaciers surged much farther out than they do today. V-shaped valleys were carved out and U-shaped dry dales built up. After the ice melted, 150 mountain lakes formed in the heart of Hohe Tauern, jewels that contain and feed the pure water of the high mountains. In the Gletschertore hundreds of small streams have their source. When the snow and ice melt in spring and summer, small mountain streams hurl themselves down with great force and form spectacular waterfalls. The Krimmler Waterfalls, with a total height of 380 metres, are the highest in Europe.

Where the glaciers have withdrawn, a fast-changing landscape reveals itself. First there are the moraines, formed by glacial ice, but quite soon pioneering plants begin to appear. A wild primal landscape exists next to the cultivated landscape created by farmers. That is the twofold history of Hohe Tauern. After the latest Ice Age – 10,000 years ago – Hohe Tauern formed a desert of rocks, rubble and grit. Very slowly animals and plants populated the new living space – particularly species from the cold Central Asiatic steppes, the polar regions and the Siberian tundra. First they inhabited the valleys and then, as the temperature began to rise, they followed the glacier as it withdrew high into the mountains. In the valley the forest returned with birches from the Balkans, and larches and pine trees from the Asiatic taiga. And so gradually the typical Alpine vegetation zones developed. A journey from the valley to the mountains is equivalent to a 4,000 kilometre journey to polar regions. A third of all plant species found in Austria and about 10,000 animal species live in Hohe Tauern.

It is winter here for eight months of the year. Spring and autumn are hardly noticeable. Many species of animals have adapted to this in their physique, physiology and behaviour. Consequently they can survive only here. In the summer Hohe Tauern exudes an enormous vitality. A sea of flowers colours the landscape and attracts insects for pollination. Ptarmigans assemble for their courtship, marmots sun themselves on the rocks, ravens show off stunt flights. Fauna and flora show themselves in all their glory.

Chamois and ibex

Chamois can be seen regularly. Their coat is red-brown in summer; in winter it changes to a blackish brown. Both sexes have horns. Usually the females live with their fawns in herds, led by an old goat. The make-up of the herd can change remarkably from year to year. The young bucks also form herds, while the old ones are notably solitary. Only during the mating season in November do the bucks join the female herds. Fierce fighting may then break out between rival bucks.

The ibex is a true goat and can mate with a domestic nanny goat. The females weigh 45 kilograms, the bucks often more than 100 kilograms. The buck has powerful horns, bent backwards and a metre long, while the doe has short horns, hardly bent. Ibex are strong climbers and jumpers because of their split hooves. The bucks and the does with their young live in separate herds. During the mating season in December–January the bucks look for the does and seek to control the herd. This leads to fighting among the bucks.

Vultures

Hohe Tauern is the only area in the Alps where wild vultures occur regularly. Between May and September more than thirty griffons live here. These scavengers spend the summer in Hohe Tauern, but they do not breed there. Any white-headed vultures in the park at any other time are probably younger birds who are not breeding yet, or older ones who have mated without results. White-headed vultures live in groups. They nest year after year in traditional sleeping places in the Rauriser- and Hollersbachtal.

The lammergeier – with a wingspan of up to 2.9 metres – is one of the largest birds when flying. In flight lammergeiers are identifiable by their pendant wings and tail and by their head, which points downwards. Adult lammergeiers have a plumage full of contrasts. The top side is a blackish grey; the head, neck and underside are white to a pinkish red. The red colour comes from bathing in mud containing iron. This vulture is remarkable for the black feathers over its beak. Lammergeiers nest in niches in the rocks. Their 'hunting grounds' stretch out between 100 and 750 square kilometres. Within that area a breeding pair has a vast territory, which it protects against invaders. The lammergeier lives on carrion. A large part of the birds' food (up to 90 per cent) consists of bones, which they digest completely. Lammergeiers drop large bones down on the rocks from a height, so that they break up into edible pieces.

Golden eagle

The golden eagle has a wingspan of 2.2 metres. Older birds get very dark, while young birds stand out for the white flecks on their wings and their white tails with a black tip. The golden eagle owes its 'proud' look to its pronounced eye sockets. Golden eagles are monogamous and breed on rocks or in large trees. Each pair has several nests. Their nesting places are usually below the hunting ground, so that the birds can transport their prey to the nest easily. Golden eagles hunt close to the ground and try to surprise their prey at a short distance. They hunt primarily small to medium-large mammals, which they kill with their sharp beak and powerful claws. Their hunting grounds extend over 50 to 150 square kilometres.

Hohe tauern

Hohe Tauern is a long stretch of a mountain range in the middle of the central Alps in Austria. It is about 120 kilometres long from east to west, and 50 kilometres wide from north to south. Protection of the area began in 1918 and continued in phases. Typical features are large expanses of glaciers (180 km²), valleys scoured out during the Ice Age, alpine grass, heathland, and woodland with larch, spruce and pine. Fast-flowing mountain streams provide spectacular views. Hohe Tauern is the largest protected area of natural beauty (1,834 km²) in the Alps. The landscape varies from glaciers and rock faces to Alpine meadows laboriously laid out. This is the roof of Austria, with the Großglockner (3,798 metres) the highest of more than 300 peaks of 3,000 metres or more. Despite the extreme living conditions, Hohe Tauern is home to a large variety of creatures that are not found anywhere else in Austria. The Tauernfenster is a geological sensation: a geological 'window' that contains four massive cores of gneiss. Originating from flows of magma, these form famous peaks such as the Großvenediger or the Hohen Sonnblick.

INTERVIEW WITH CONSERVATIONIST GUNTHER GRESSMANN, OF HOHE TAUERN

What makes the Hohe Tauern such an exceptional area in the Alps?
In Hohe Tauern you will find the largest glaciers in the eastern Alps. The so-called Tauernfenster is very old, geological formation that is found only here and illustrates the origin of the Alps. There are exceptional relationships between animals and between flora and fauna. There is also a unique relationship between the natural area and the core region, where there is limited human activity. For instance, typical Alpine meadows are protected as an important habitat for animals and plants. Hohe Tauern is a protected area of 1,800 km² with a hunt-free zone of around 885 km².

You study the ibex. How important is that population?
At the moment there are about 1,100 ibexes in Hohe Tauern and the number is growing; there are also contacts with other populations in North and South Tyrol. Research shows that the ibex used to live in Hohe Tauern, before the animals were wiped out there. Only the golden eagle is now a threat for the young animals; they have no other natural enemies. The winter presents no great problem because there are sufficient suitable habitats.

How are the vultures doing in Hohe Tauern?
There are two kinds of vulture in Hohe Tauern. The lammergeier lives there the whole year round and the white-headed vulture stays there from spring to autumn. Hohe Tauern is a traditional summer region for white-headed vultures, which come mostly from Croatia but sometimes also from France, Spain or Israel. They feed on the dead bodies of wildlife or farm animals – for instance sheep. The number of white-headed vultures varies between 40 and 70. Most of the lammergeiers stay in Hohe Tauern throughout the year; only some not fully developed birds travel south in the winter. The number of lammergeiers varies between 18 and 22 in the summer and autumn period and between 12 and 14 in the winter and spring period. These numbers apply to the whole of Austria, because most lammergeiers live in Hohe Tauern.

Are there still wild trout?
There are indeed wild trout in some of the rivers. Currently there is a project for breeding from these. They have been reintroduced in certain distant parts of rivers in the park. You can find information about the project at http://www.hohetauern.at/de/forschung/projekte/122-forschung-projekte/494-trout-exam-invest-qurforelleq.html.

Why are the Alpine meadows being retained? What is the ecological importance of this?
In the core zone there are many Alpine meadows that are being mown by farmers in the traditional way. A very rich flora and fauna flourishes on these meadows – particularly of butterflies and beetles. On several Alpine meadows cattle graze, and this produces a very specific flora, often near traditional huts. The fauna in these zones is also very typical. For instance, the monkshood attracts special varieties of bees. To protect the area's biodiversity, the mowing of the Alpine meadows is financially supported.

◄ Glaciers, in a colour palette of white and all shades of blue. Here you can expect to see the lammergeier.

▼ Cascades of ice pour into the depths and disappear under beautiful but highly dangerous mountains.

► A primitive Alpine area, hewn from rock and ice.

SIERRA DE GUARA

SIERRA DE GUARA – CANYONS

Realm of predatory and carrion birds

An eagle owl is caught in the beam of the headlamps. With a loud whoosh it flies up from between the olive trees. Its dull-grey silhouette is surprisingly large. I am in vulture land. There are an estimated 6,000 of these birds in Spain. They nest high up against the rocky walls in the canyons. I can see a large number of red kites and a few rare Bonelli eagles. I'm moving between seas of olive groves and almond trees. The soil is ochre in colour, the sunset blinding.

Wild vultures take off and land on a steep rock wall. When I see a couple 20 metres away I sense that they are screening me. This is clearly no place for anyone suffering from a fear of heights. Round the peaks blows a strong wind on which the birds let themselves be carried. A young lammergeier and an imperial eagle hang together in the sky. Lammergeiers and ravens cross each other's paths and then each go their separate ways. Their wingspan varies between 1.2 and 2.8 metres. From a distance their silhouettes look similar. The mountains are like gigantic molars, filled with birds. Songbirds feed themselves with the abundant insects and in turn are hunted by the birds of prey. An imperial eagle is being followed by two ravens, floating just above its tail, frightened of being attacked by this top bird of prey. A lammergeier drops a bone on a rock, and then crushes the pieces with its imposing beak.

Sierra de Guara

The Sierra de Guara has three main canyons with many small side branches. The ground consists of porous lime and sandstone. Water and wind have free play here. This has created the most beautiful variations in the landscape. Canyons result from shifts in the Earth's crust and erosion. In some places the Earth's crust is torn open. These tears are filled with water. Erosion then gets a grip on the landscape and wears down a new canyon. In places where the Earth's crust has risen wind, water and glaciers have an opportunity to form canyons. The wind only has free play once a start has been made. Water wears down a piece of the landscape bit by bit. In sedimentary stone this happens faster than in granite. In areas where the ground consists mainly of sandstone and lime, wind and water have even freer play. Rounder stones develop than would be the case among harder kinds of stone. In this respect the Sierra de Guara is like the Grand Canyon in America.

Situated on the south side of the Pyrenees, the Sierra de Guara enjoys a microclimate. Moist air from the north collides with the mountain range. The French side of the Pyrenees is much damper than the Spanish. It is easy to see this from the difference in vegetation. The higher parts of the Guara are on the western side and these hold the damp air back from the Atlantic Ocean.

Consequently the area is very dry and enjoys many hours of sunshine. October and April are the wettest months. The temperature in winter is about 9°C in the daytime and about –10°C at night. In summer the temperature goes up to 35°C. The nights are considerably cooler, but the temperature does not drop below 17°C.

Vultures

The biggest vulture around here is the griffon. It is 1 metre long and has a wingspan of 3 metres. With a weight of 10 to 15 kilograms it lets itself be driven on the wind. In ideal living conditions it can live for sixty years. The Egyptian vulture is a smaller, quite common species. An Egyptian vulture can spot an 8-centimetres-long victim from a height of 1,000 metres. It can live for about thirty-five years and is faithful to its partner for life. The lammergeier is the most threatened species of vulture in Europe. Nicknamed 'bonecrusher', it chases its prey against the rock wall or drives it into a ravine. Farmers have almost exterminated this species by putting poisoned meat on the dumping places for carrion, on which they feed.

Meanwhile a European regulation threatens the future of the vulture. Traditionally they feed themselves with the remains of carrion collected at the edge of villages. But health and safety regulations dictate that carrion may no longer be left in the open air. Environmental organizations are opposing the regulation and trying to keep open the carrion pits, where hundreds of kilograms of bones wait for eager vultures to clean the carcasses.

Canyons form an ideal breeding site for vultures, and in Sierra de Guara there are still many species. But because increasingly farmers no longer leave their cattle to roam free in the mountains, and because the carrion pits are being closed, the vultures are threatened by famine. Consequently they need another source of food. If they do not find this the vultures will – at least temporarily – have to go elsewhere to look for food. That is why a few years ago some hundred vultures from Spain suddenly turned up in Belgium and the Netherlands, never having been seen before in these northern countries.

▶ *This pair of vultures is waiting for a favourable thermal on which to launch themselves into the void.*

▼ A colony of griffons passes the night on the cliffs. Here they rest, tidy their feathers, stretch themselves out, quarrel, mate . . . A world of feathers and down.

▲   In protest against a law, some goatherds turned loose thousands of goats. Now the animals are potential prey for vultures.

◄   The canyons of Aragon: a monumental land-scape.

▼   Learn to fly by falling and getting up again: a young vulture practises in the wind.

▼▼   Aragon offers landscapes you would not expect to see in Europe. The principle of trans-humance does not apply here, which is a problem for the various species of vultures.

▼▼▼   Such a spectacle from primitive times is a daily occurrence here.

HELLAS

DADIA – PRESPA – EVROS

DADIA – MEDITERRANEAN FOREST

WHERE TORTOISES FALL OUT OF THE SKY

On the path I find the shell of a tortoise. Fragments of the shell lie to left and right. What drama has taken place here? I am told that in the Greek Dadia forest the golden eagle hunts tortoises. Its hunting technique reminds me of the lammergeier. The beautiful bird of prey grabs a tortoise, flies away with it, higher and higher, and finally drops its prey on the rocks to crack the shell. Then it immediately dives after its prey to pick out the meat. It's only here that the eagles employ this hunting technique. Have the birds learnt it by observing scavengers? Or is it the result of trial and error?

The carcass of a cow is food for vultures. A snake's tail dangles from the beak of a short-toed eagle taking it to its young. I can see a nest of black vultures, and a little farther on in the water a few square metres of tadpoles surrounded by clumps of frogs and turtles with plump limbs. The rivers are full of freshwater crayfish. Honey buzzards fly to and fro. I walk past the squashed remains of a huge snake with a lizard in its belly. The area is teeming with black storks.

Dadia

The Dadia-Leukimi-Soufli zone (up to 1,650 metres) has been protected since 1980. The villages in the area have 11,000 inhabitants, mainly active in agriculture, stock breeding, forestry and ecotourism. Rivers course through the woods. Two dams ensure a permanent supply of water for the stock.

The rich forests of Dadia near the town of Alexandroupolis in northern Greece form a rest and foraging area along an important migration route for birds. Dadia is one of the places where rare birds of prey and vultures, such as the black vulture and the Egyptian vulture, hunt and breed. The forest protects the vultures during the long breeding period. Dadia is a classic example of a Mediterranean ecosystem, which has developed over centuries through the symbiosis of man and nature. Mainly conifers and oaks grow here. The forest is interrupted at intervals by open spaces and agriculture. This patchwork quilt of landscape forms an ideal habitat for birds of prey. You can find thirty-six of the thirty-eight European birds of prey here, among them the rare imperial eagle and the lesser spotted eagle. Also three of the four European species of vulture – the black vulture, Egyptian vulture and bearded vulture – are all found here.

The black vulture is a notable sight in the forest. Dadia has the only breeding colony in Greece and the Balkans, and one of the last in Europe. The population consists of some 100 specimens, including twenty breeding pairs. Occasionally the birds are fed, but never enough to make them dependent. In the long run they have to keep to their predatory habits and look for their food in the forest.

INTERVIEW WITH CONSERVATIONIST YANNIS MARINOS, OF WWF EVROS

How many golden eagles are there in the park? Can you describe their typical behaviour?
According to the latest survey there are five or six breeding couples. Because of its enormous wingspan it is almost impossible for the golden eagle to hunt between the trees of the dense forest. Its ideal hunting territory is in open zones and around the cliffs. Research tells us that an important part of its diet consists of turtles and tortoises, particularly the Hermann's tortoise (Testudo hermanni) and the Moorish tortoise (Testudo graeca). The golden eagle has developed an interesting method of hunting. When it circles above the park, it can easily find and grab turtles and tortoises. Then it uses the warm air currents to drive it to a great height and looks for a rocky area. It drops the animal and immediately takes an impressive dive down with it, so that it does not lose sight of its prey. The shell is shattered against the rocks.

DADIA NATIONAL PARK

In 2006 a zone of 42,800 hectares was declared a national park, of which 7,800 hectares are subject to strict protection and the rest a buffer zone. There are 219 species of birds in the Dadia National Park. The rich population of birds of prey in particular is exceptional for such a relatively small area. The lesser spotted eagle and the short-toed eagle, also known as the snake eagle, are more numerous here than elsewhere in Greece. There is also an important population of black storks. Furthermore, 29 species of reptile and 12 species of amphibian have been observed, most of which are protected. There are 63 species of mammal in the area, including 24 protected species of bat. Because of the position of the park on the border between Europe and Asia, it is on the edge of the distribution area for species from both sides. For north European bird species – the Isabelline wheatear and the masked shrike, for instance – this is the most southern distribution area. There are also Asiatic species that in Europe are only found in Thrace and the Evros region. The most southerly distribution area of the European meadow lizard and the fire-bellied toad is in Thrace, while Asiatic species, such as the rock viper and the snake-eyed lizard, do not occur farther west.

▲   The tortoise hides in hollows, well protected against the sun.

▶   This beauty (Dracunculus vulgaris) uses an indescribable smell of rot to attract insects.

▲　*This oakwood valley teems with birds.*

▶　*Not a snake, not a lizard, but a blindworm. He always manages to save himself at the last moment, with a lot of noise.*

▶▶　*Wasps build a nest of cellulose, inconspicuous and at first sight totally innocent.*

▶▶▶　*Prey for the short-toed eagle. I saw the eagle swallow the 1 -metre-long snake, leaving the moving tail dangling from its beak.*

▶▶▶▶　*On the ground there is a small world buzzing with life.*

PRESPA – BALKAN LAKES

Reed collars around one of the oldest lakes in Europe

In the heart of the Balkans I get a whiff of the Middle East. Time seems to stand still here. Asian water buffaloes graze the reeds along the banks of the Prespa lakes. Huge dogs protect the buffalo, sheep and goats against wolves and bears. Droppings in the street show that bears regularly go round the villages. There is a rehabilitation centre (called Arcturos) in the area for bears that have managed to escape from circus performers. Scientists from the centre follow the bears with radio telemetry. They examine the places where they scratch themselves and carry out DNA tests on the hairs they find.

All around is water and mountains, with oceans of reed stems, 6 to 7 metres high, waving in the wind. The reed beds are a nursery for the fish that spawn there. Later these fish look for deeper waters, where they are targeted by the Dalmatian pelican, the little egret and the dwarf cormorant. In the south the lake goes on into Macedonia and Albania. I watch an enormous flock of ducks and coots, flying low and forming a new horizon. The clouds are reflected in the enormous lakes. The sun dries out the ground. The play of light is magical. A peregrine swoops close above my head. The mountains make a splendid outline against the sky, clouds sticking to them like candy floss.

On the banks of the lake the geese tolerate me, but the coots immediately take off. A buzzard hangs above the edge of the reed, flies up and dives down again. Two young sparrowhawks ascend, like spirits, crossing each other's paths. They go on upwards and vanish from my sight, high in the air. The reed bed is an impenetrable labyrinth. I clamber to the top of a hill and on the way find the shell of a tortoise among the shrubs.

The Prespa lakes

The Prespa lakes lie along the frontier of Albania and the former Yugoslav republic of Macedonia. The Prespa National Park is enclosed by several mountain massifs. To the left of the park are the Albanian mountains and to the right the peak of Vermion (2,128 metres). The area (2,519 km²) is known for its rich biodiversity. There is a large breeding colony of Dalmatian pelicans. In the isolated, 850-metre-high basin, in which the Prespa lakes originated in the Tertiary period, a unique ecosystem developed, hardly disturbed by man. A large number of water birds feel at home there, among them the dwarf cormorant, the common cormorant, the bee-eater, the great crested grebe, the hoopoe, the reed warbler, the night heron, the purple egret, the great and the little white egret, the black-headed bunting, the pink pelican, the rare Dalmatian pelican and the osprey. Pollution and intensive use of water for farming have had a significant effect. Now the WWF and its partners protect the region with a number of initiatives, among them conservation, environmental education and the promotion of sustainable development projects.

INTERVIEW WITH CONSERVATIONIST IRENE KOUTSERI, OF THE SOCIETY FOR THE PROTECTION OF PRESPA

How does the ecosystem work with the reed beds and the wetlands?

During floods the short species of grass in the wet grassland on the banks of the Prespa lake are submerged. This is the domain of amphibians. Fish come here to spawn and water birds, such as the dwarf cormorant and the Dalmatian pelican, forage here. The reed beds are traditionally managed by farmers. Since grazing was abandoned and the cutting and use of reed was stopped, the wet grasslands have been limited in extent. The growth of reed is not controlled and the reed beds are extending farther into the land. The Society for the Protection of Prespa started the regeneration of the wet grasslands with the introduction of a small number of water buffaloes in 1997. Water buffaloes and cows were used for grazing and the reed was cut every summer. In this way the surface area of the wet grassland increased from 32.5 hectares to 100 hectares. Local farmers and fishermen were involved in the project. The farmers saw the yield of hay expand appreciably; the fishermen saw the fish stock (particularly of carp) increase. The water buffaloes play an important role in the management of wet grasslands, because they eat the young reed shoots in the spring and in this way limit the spread of the reeds. This has proved to be the most effective way of maintaining the wet grassland. In the areas that were grazed by buffaloes the reed was replaced faster by wet meadow plants. Moreover, water birds used these zones more intensively.

Why is there such large population of Dalmatian pelicans and dwarf cormorants?

The largest colony of Dalmatian pelicans (20 per cent of the world population, 1,100 couples) lives by the Prespa lakes. In the early 1990s there were only 200 couples. Dalmatian pelicans eat fish which they catch in shallow water, for instance in wetlands. This is because they can't dive into deep water. They build their nests in the reed beds. The dwarf cormorants also live on fish. They too make up the largest colony in Europe. The area of lakes turns out to be extremely suitable as a foraging and breeding area for these birds. There is also a small population of grey geese, the only breeding population in Greece. This species is common in northern

◄ *Very dense reed beds make an ideal breeding area for fish. The dwarf cormorant keeps watch. It is perfectly adapted to this biotope.*

Europe, but the population in Prespa appears to be isolated from other populations.

How do you explain the exceptional biodiversity in this region?

Prespa is an isolated region, a natural depression with the lakes in the deepest part, surrounded by high mountains (as explained in Prespa: A Story for Man and Nature by G. Catsadorakis). The surrounding mountains reach heights of more than 2,300 metres, while the lakes are at an altitude of 850 metres. The great difference in altitudes creates an enormous variety of habitats, from alpine meadows to sub-alpine shrubberies, beech and oak woods, an agricultural zone around the villages, and wetlands and reed beds in the lower regions. Moreover, the geology is very varied. The eastern side of the Varnous consists of impenetrable granite. There are rivers and streams there. The Devas and Vrondero mountains in the west and the Sfika in the south are formed of permeable limestone. Here there are no rivers. Consequently the vegetation differs according to the geology (underground). Prespa is one of the coldest areas of Greece, but the climate is milder than in nearby Florina (because of the presence of water). The vegetation is a combination of central European and Mediterranean species. Finally, human presence has played an important role in the preservation of the various habitats. All these factors have combined created a unique biodiversity, with more than 1,400 plant species, a large number of breeding birds, 44 species of mammal and 8 indigenous fish species.

Why do pelicans fly at a low level, so that they almost touch the water?

Flying near the earth's surface reduces resistance and increases the output of the wing. By means of this aerodynamic phenomenon – known as the 'ground effect' – the birds save a great deal of energy. Birds like the pelican make use of this ground effect to an unusual extent. Some even touch the waves with their wing tips.

▲ The Balkans and the Prespa lakes. There are still bears here. During the night they visit the villages; their droppings are evidence of their predatory raids.

▲▲ Grey geese on their way to nearby Albania.

▲ The management of the reed beds has for years been beneficial to the local economy.

▲   *Buffaloes, imported from Asia and integrated here, maintain the reed beds.*

▲ *The middle of the reed beds teems with life.*

▶ *The heavy flight of a pelican. The oldest birds do not migrate any more.*

▼ *A sky like this invites you to explore and to meditate.*

EVROS – DELTA AND LAGOON

ON THE BORDER BETWEEN FRESH AND SALT WATER

There are too many birds here to be counted. For every wasp there is an army of wasp-eating honey buzzards, and I can also see many black storks. A sea of flowers stretches out before my eyes. Ospreys circle high in the sky. Is that a jackal howling? On the ground there are enormous threatening spiders, ants and centipedes, 20 centimetres long. Suddenly a bright yellow snake darts off like lightning and climbs into a tree. When I touch its tail it coils up like a spring. The snake protects itself against its natural enemy, the snake eagle. Meanwhile the song of the night-ingale fills the valley. It is enchanting. I pick up a tortoise from the ground and remove the ticks from its body. In this transitional zone where man and beast live together, it is easy to observe. I don't have to plan anything; every situation offers itself sponta-neously. I see the tortoise and the centipede (they sound like one of Aesop's fables) beside each other, two monsters. The snake eagle searches the ground. Two butterflies mate while one is being eaten by a spider. How to make love while facing death! Twenty metres farther on a large snake shoots away. It is a slow-worm, a lizard without feet. A swarm of hornets hangs in the air. There are wasp nests between the flowers.

We are sailing through the delta to the islands. Among the algae eggs are hidden. We see the body of a beached dolphin, its mouth twisted in an eternal grin. The sky is white with terns, swans, pelicans and egrets. An island is populated by cormorants. A riverbed is almost dry, a paradise for black storks. It teems with turtles. High above me a Balkan sparrowhawk circles. A mass of dragonflies, golden orioles and glossy ibises, reptiles and amphi-bians, in large numbers. Tortoises have dug out their hidey-holes. I can see processions of larvae. I am looking on at a display of eating and being eaten. I haven't enough eyes to see it all. There is no end to it. Everything is beautiful and exceptionally varied. I see a number of situations in a single glance in the clear, fresh water of the lagoon, 40 kilometres from the Turkish border.

The Evros delta

The Evros delta (188 km²) near the frontier with Turkey is an area of great ecological importance. The Evros is the second largest ri-ver in Eastern Europe. Rising in the Rila mountains in Bulgaria, its basin stretches between the Rodopi and the Ainos mountain ran-ges. The Evros is 528 kilometres long, of which 310 kilometres are in Bulgaria and 218 kilometres on the frontiers of Greece, Bulgaria and Turkey. The total river basin covers an area of 53.000 km², of which 66.2 per cent is in Bulgaria, 27.5 per cent in Turkey and 6.3 per cent in Greece. The flow varies between 8 m³ per second and 100 m³ per second. A mass of sediments is deposited in the Evros delta. The climate in the delta is predominantly Mediterranean, but continental influences also play a part. The winter is harsh and it often freezes from the beginning of winter till late in spring. Rain falls randomly over the whole year, but the summers are mostly dry.

The Evros delta is the most important biotope in Greece for three European varieties of swan: the mute swan, the whooper swan and the Bewick swan. In the wet grasslands thousands of white-fronted geese forage in the winter, together with hundreds of red-breasted geese. Almost all the European breeding populations of the threatened dwarf geese stay for weeks in the wet grasslands before they start on their great spring trek to their breeding grounds in the north. Particularly during the winter rare birds of prey can be seen: the spotted eagle, the imperial eagle and the white-tail-ed eagle are regular visitors then. Other important bird species are the Dalmatian pelican, the dwarf cormorant, the bittern, the ferruginous duck, the red kite, the spoonbill, the black ibis and the collared pratincole.

The Evros delta is one of the most important wet grasslands, not only in Greece but also in Europe. Because of its great importance to a number of bird species, 9,500 hectares of land and 1,500 hectares of water are protected under the Ramsar Convention. In the first half of the twentieth century the Evros delta remained unchanged. The cycle of erosion and deposit between the sea, river and land and the influence of the waves on the coast have contributed to a dynamic ecosystem. However, this natural cycle was affected by human intervention. Between 1950 and 1980 dams, canals, dikes, flood defences and irrigation works changed the delta. The government also wanted to expand agricultural land. The freshwater supply decreased, the inflow of fresh water in the delta region was limited and seawater overflowed into the heart of the delta. After the completion of the works a large part of the morasses and wet grasslands was drained. In the end the drainage of the delta resulted in no productive agricultural land because of the increased salinization of the land in the south-western delta.

In 1987 farmers closed the entrance of the Drana lagoon, believing that the lagoon was responsible for the salinization of the tilled farmland. This action led to the degradation of the habitat in the lagoon. Colonies of fish and fowl breeding around the islands in the lagoon disappeared. Draining the Drana lagoon did not benefit the farmers. Moreover, the delta lost an important habitat and – equally important – a profitable fish stock. After ten years the local community decided to restore the lagoon to its natural state.

▲ A cloud of tadpoles – a delicious meal for many predators.

▲▲ Shelducks come in to land.

▶ A perfect example of design and mimetism. I have to be attentive with every step.

▲ *During migration an innumerable number of birds spend time in the delta.*

▲ *A turtle hides himself, its neck as tense as a spring. The prey has been warned.*

▲ The turtle conserves heat – essential energy for hunting. I noticed that sometimes turtles spend up to twenty minutes under water.

▼ Cormorants. Walking through a wall of cries, I travelled through all phases of life.

▼▼ A stranded dolphin.

▼ *A fertile soup. This is the richest ecosystem I visited, a unique microcosm.*

▶ *A flight of waders. They look like cotton wool, carried by the wind.*

▶ *Another example of mimetism: the colour of the eggs makes them almost invisible.*

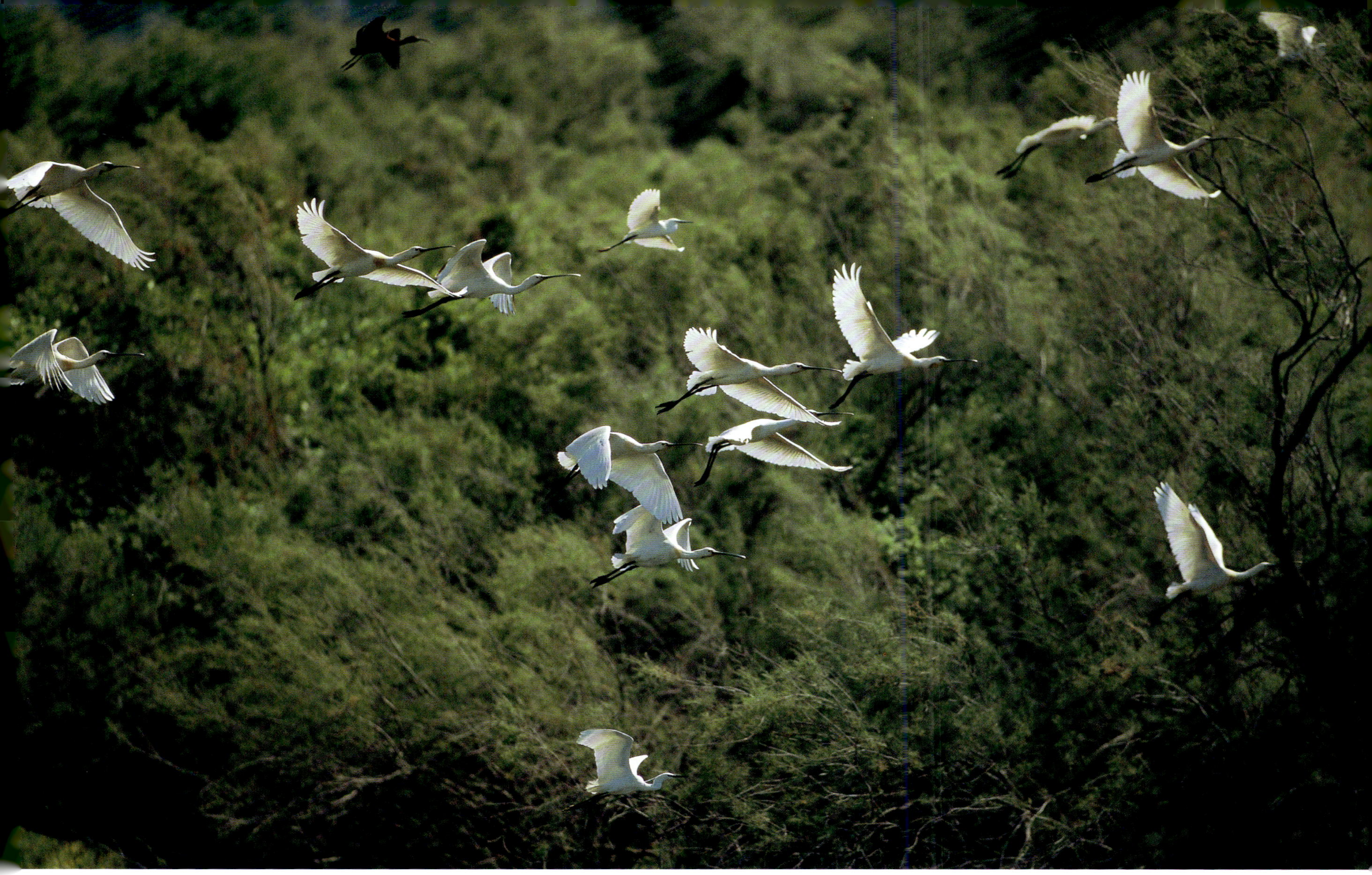

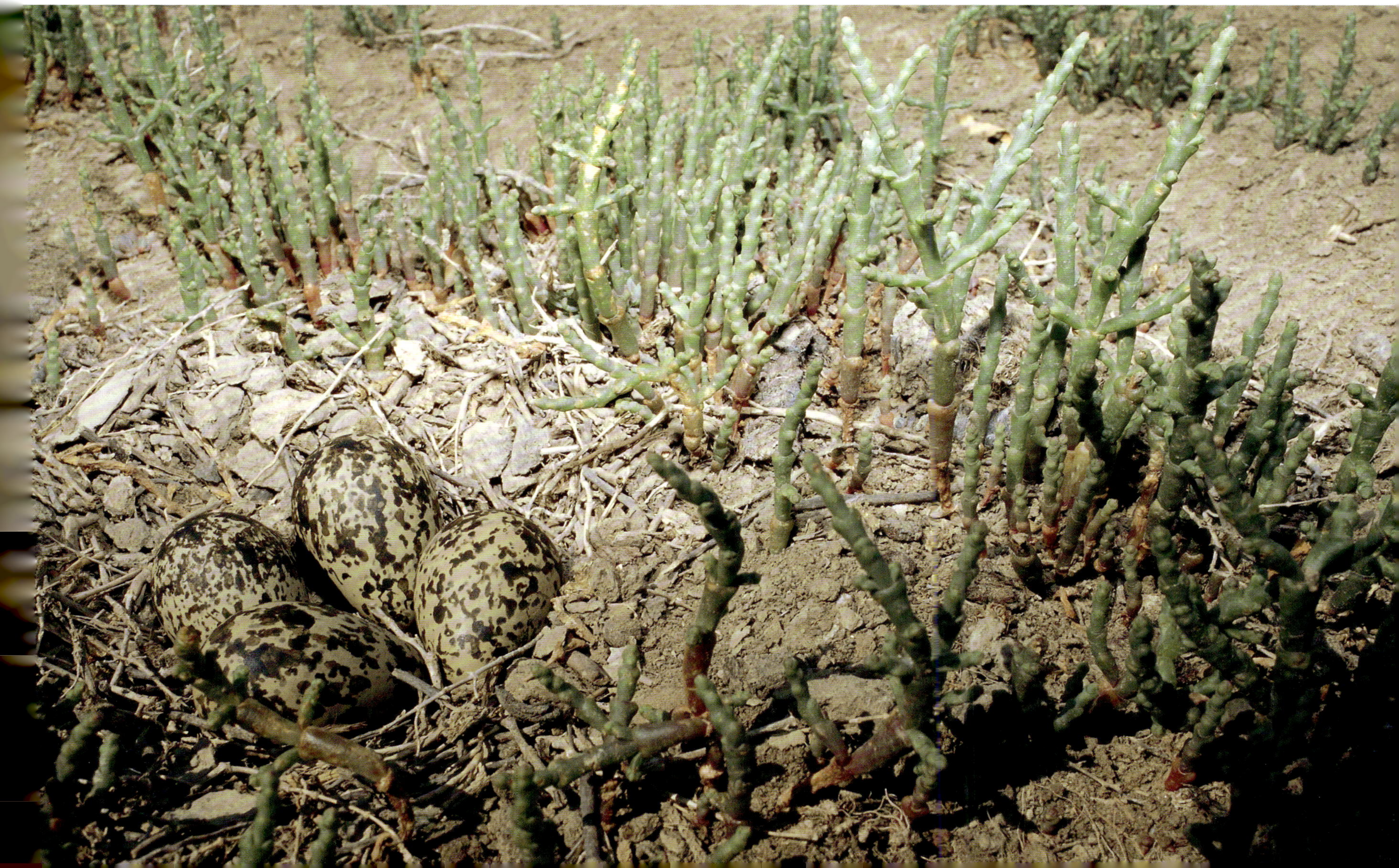

SLOVENIJA

KROKAR

KROKAR – MIXED WOODLAND

A GAME OF PICK UP STICKS WITH BEARS

In the woods of south-western Slovenia there are brown bears. This is no accident, because these woods have been well protected for years. The tops of the mountains here on the border with Croatia (1,000 metres) are entirely virgin territory; I can find no trace of exploitation or tourism there. Consequently the biodiversity is outstanding. For years access to this territory was strictly forbidden because of its strategic importance militarily and the area was closed off during the Cold War. Even now, you still need official permission to enter this wood. In Krokar four fragments of woodland together form a giant game of pick up sticks with trees that have fallen across and on top of each other. In an area of 100 hectares there are magnificent woods where rotting tree trunks are not cleared away. Krokar (meaning crow) is an uncultivated primeval forest. Trees that show signs of attack by wood beetle are left to nature. Dead wood is particularly important for biodiversity, as a dead tree often contains more life than a living one.

I enjoy the fantastic view, a panorama of 360 degrees all round. Actually, I would have preferred to fly over this part, so as not to put a stone out of place. Everything here fits perfectly, as in the ultimate aesthetic experience. I keep finding rotten tree trunks in my way, attacked by woodpeckers. Occasionally I fall. If I stop for a moment, my body is immediately covered with a carpet of flies. Over time a symbiosis between man and beast has developed here. Only when the bears go beyond the boundaries of their territory and migrate outside the wood – for instance, to plunder orchards – do they meet problems.

After waiting for a long time, I see the first bears in the woods. The scene looks like an etching by Hainard, the Swiss animal artist. This is no coincidence, because he made the same observation here. A brown bear is swallowing small stones to help his digestion. He shakes a fallen tree as if it were a swing and this seems to amuse him. There is a clear hierarchy among bears. When, soon, a second one arrives, the lightest one briefly looks up and pricks up its ears; then there is a growl. My observation of them is interrupted by heavy rainfall. Thunder and lightning introduce a dramatic note to the idyllic scene. The noise reminds me that I am in the realm of bears and it is in my interest to respect their rules. Watching some more, I see three young bears. For a brief moment the tension rises; then the animals calm down again. A female bear appears with two cubs beside her. She blows and growls a little, possibly to warn me. The three middle-sized bears disappear again. There are no signs of conflict. Slowly night falls. I should have left my hide earlier, I realize, but with a mother bear and cubs around, the spectacle was so fascinating that night crept up on me.

Later, in the light of the jeep's headlights, I see the silhouette of a marten, dragging a hare along. He runs away, but will undoubtedly come back soon to collect his prey.

Slovenia

Slovenia, situated in the south-eastern Alps and the northern Balkans, is a small country (20,000 km^2), about 55 per cent of it covered with forest and hence the third most heavily wooded country in the European Union. About 85 per cent regenerates naturally, so that native species of trees are preserved and genetic diversity promoted. Large uninterrupted areas of woodland offer space to specialized woodland animals, such as the bear and the lynx. There are forty recognized reserves, four of them with uncultivated primeval forest (1.25 per cent of the forested area).

Slovenia lies on the north-western boundary of the distribution area of the Eurasian brown bear in the Dinaric and eastern Alps. There is a stable population of 320 to 400 bears spread over 5,000 km^2, particularly in the forested southern regions along the Croatian frontier. The Alpine and pre-Alpine regions in West Slovenia form an essential link for the expansion of the brown bears from the Dinaric mountains to the Alps. The brown bear occurs in the large wooded areas in the eastern Alps, in the north-east of Italy and in the Pindus mountains in Greece. The habitat of the population in south Slovenia consists of thick beech and spruce woods. The region is linked to the Gorski-Kotar plateau in Croatia. The bear population hère is growing and is also spreading to more westerly areas. Between 1972 and 1997 there was a great deal of fear and resistance among the local population, who were not used to bears. Sheep were regularly killed by the bears. In 1993 the government approved the Protection of Endangered Species Act, by which the brown bear acquired the status of a protected animal – and in the Alps too, despite the protests of the local inhabitants.

Triglav National Park (TNP) is the only national park in Slovenia in the north of the country. It was named after the highest mountain, Triglav (2,864 metres). The park extends along the Italian border and along the Austrian border in the north-west of Slovenia (south-eastern Alps). The terrain is much the same as that of the eastern Julian Alps. The park (880 km²) occupies 3 per cent of the country's surface area. The protection goes back to 1924. The most striking features of the landscape are valleys scoured out by glaciers, mountain plateaux and high mountains above the tree line. The park takes pride in its pure water, deeply cut gorges, remains of primeval forest, rich biodiversity and an Eldorado of mountain flowers, among them the native campanula and the alpine poppy. Chamois, ibex, red deer, brown bear and lynx are found here too. Altogether there are more than 5,500 species of plants and animals.

INTERVIEW WITH FRENCH BIOLOGIST JEAN-CLAUDE GENOT, WHO REGULARLY MONITORS THE BEARS IN KROKAR AND ITS SURROUNDINGS

How does such a small country come to have an important bear population?

It was a political choice to make the southern part of the country the core of bear conservation. As early as the 1970s a protected zone was set up in the neighbourhood of Kocevie, where the largest bear population lives. There is also another, less extensive population in Triglav. The population in the Dinaric Alps and the Balkans is estimated at 2,500, of which 400 are in Slovenia, 500 in Croatia, 120 in Greece, 700 in Bulgaria, 200 in Macedonia and 250 in Albania. The bear population in the Carpathians (Slovakia, Romania, Poland and Ukraine) is estimated at 8,000, with a maximum in Romania of 6,600 individuals. (Source: Living with Bears by Krystufek, Flajsman & Griffiths, 2003)

The polar bear is threatened with extinction. What fate awaits the brown bear?

The brown bear does not have so much to fear from the results of global warming but is rather the victim of an intolerant population and deforestation, which limits its hunting area and causes its food resources to dwindle.

Is there still primeval forest in Krokar?

The forest is not so old, but it is mixed. There is a great deal of brushwood and undergrowth, which flourishes on a subsoil of lime. That explains the rich biodiversity.

▶ A Syrian spotted woodpecker.

▼ Fragments of primeval forest, where death nourishes new life.

▼▼ A bear plays around like a rope dancer. He disappears when a she-bear arrives with her cub.

▲ Bears come and go. They sprint faster than dogs.

▶ *Primitive fears assault you when you get lost here.*

TÜRKIYE

ÇORUH

ÇORUH – HIGH PLATEAUX AND VALLEYS

AT THE SOURCES OF THE TIGRIS AND THE EUPHRATES

I am in the river basin of the Tigris, Euphrates and Çoruh in the far east of Turkey, close to the frontiers of Russia, Iran and Syria, enjoying splendid views of the mountains and valleys coloured red in the evening sun. The shadows of lammergeiers are gliding across the mountainsides; jackals are chasing susliks (ground squirrels); buzzards are attacking these rodents from the sky. The surroundings are breathtaking. There are spectacular, enclosed canyons. Mist hangs round the mountaintops; the valleys look like steaming Turkish baths. A covering of snow shows up pinkish under a thin layer of sand blown in from Syria. On the mountainsides someone has placed beehives. When night falls, the rivers resemble silver garlands, coloured by the moon.

I meet people who catch young sparrowhawks and train them for falconry. In the autumn sparrowhawks migrate from Russia to Arab countries via Turkey, and during the migration they are captured. The practice is very popular. Many families have a 'hunting bird', to catch partridges and quails over a six-month period. They release it again after the hunting season.

It pays for hikers to be vigilant here. The sound of barking never stops. Herdsmen protect their sheep against wolves with large Kangal dogs, which do not drive the herd but patrol among them. The Kangal is one of the few dogs that can maul a wolf.

We cover enormous distances in the vicinity of Iran. I would very much like to explore the other side of the border, but there is no time for that now. The landscape, populated with storks and Egyptian vultures, is veined and shimmering in the drought. The azure-blue water of Lake Van looks inviting, but it is apparently too salty for fish.

Çoruh

The river Çoruh in the east of Turkey rises in the Mescit mountains (3,225 metres) and flows out into the Black Sea in Georgia. The Çoruh valley is recognized as a zone that is exceptional in its biodiversity. This unique biodiversity is the result of the great differences in altitude (up to 3,000 metres) between the lowest and the highest points. This causes substantial climate changes – and changes in the fauna and flora – within relatively small zones. But the ecological system is at the moment under pressure from the large-scale building of dams. The Çoruh River Development Plan in fact includes the construction of thirteen dams.

Çoruh is situated in the western Caucasus. The landscape includes mountains, alpine meadows and deep canyons scoured out by the river and its tributaries. The valleys have a Mediterranean to an occasionally subtropical climate, with flowers, shrubs, figs and olive trees, rice fields, coniferous woods and alpine meadows. Of the plants 104 threatened species have been counted, of which 67 are indigenous. The eye-catchers among the plants are the many species of orchid, geranium, campanula and wild iris. The region is on an important migration route of various species of bird. Apart from the migratory birds you will see, among others, the lammergeier, the griffon, the black vulture, the Caucasian black grouse and the Caspian mountain grouse. In addition the area is known for the enormous variety of its butterflies. Among large mammals you will find the brown bear, the chamois, the bezoars goat, the wolf, the wildcat and the Eurasian lynx.

▶ *The surroundings are breathtaking. My vision slides over spectacular enclosed canyons.*

▼ *Wolves and coyotes are plentiful here. It pays to be vigilant*

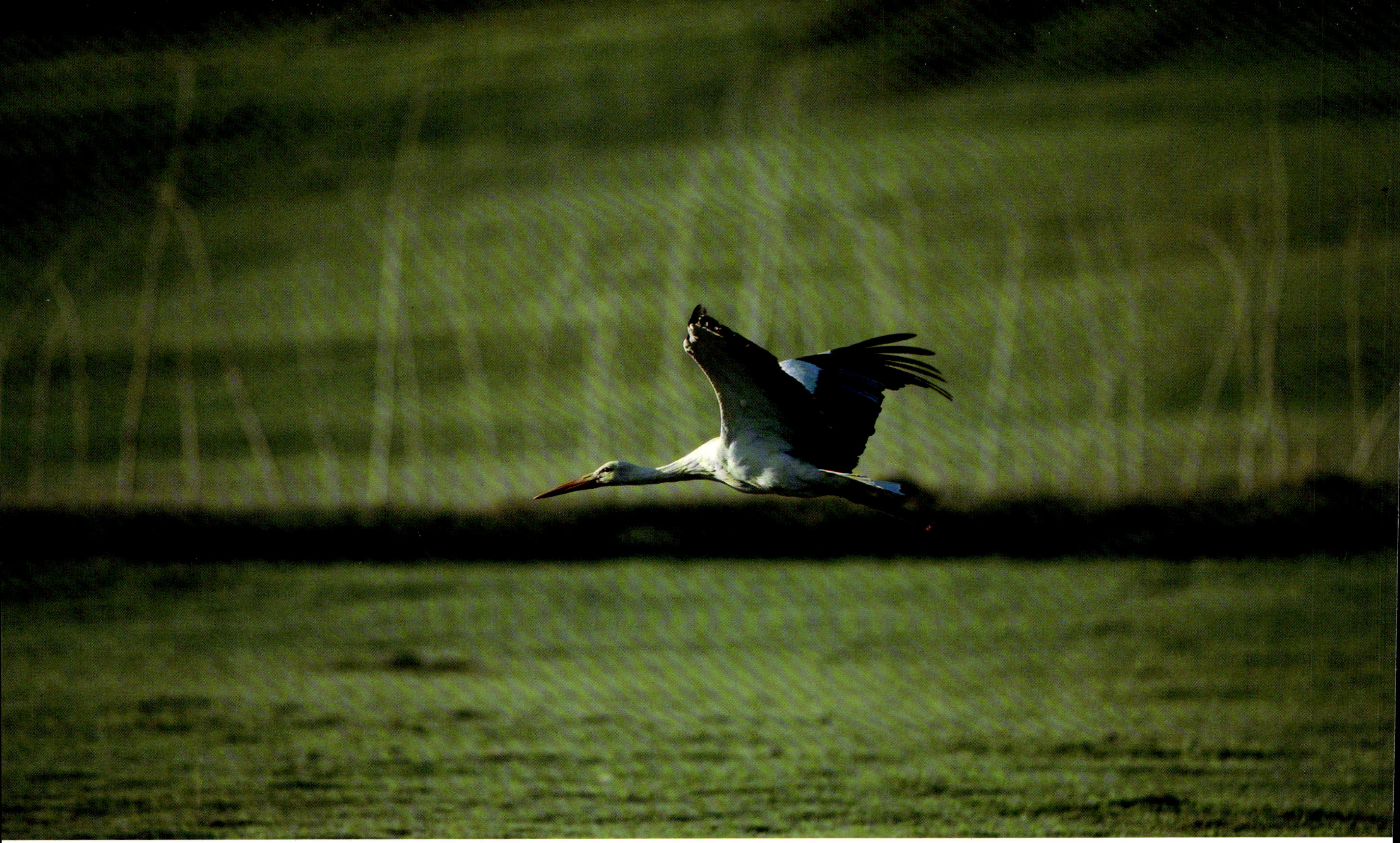

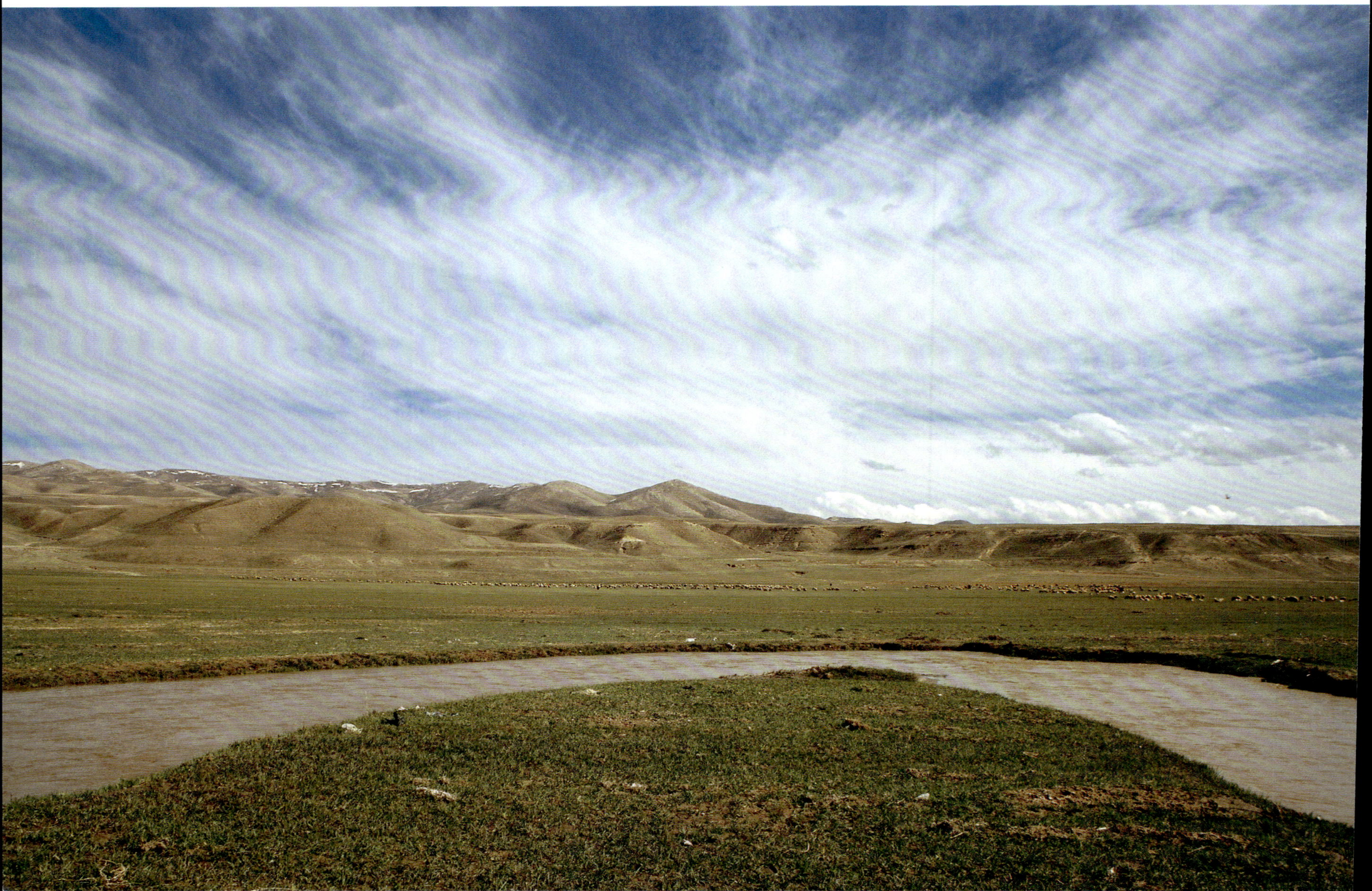

▲   Here erosion has produced pillars up to 20 metres high.

◄   The stork, an indefatigable traveller, like a great, white cross in the sky.

◄◄   The Tigris and Euphrates region. In the light of the moon the rivers become garlands of silver.

▼   Traditionally the European sparrowhawk is captured during its migration, tamed and trained to hunt. After a few months it is let loose again.

◄ Herdsmen enter the domain of the wolf. Wolves detect them, investigate and go on the prowl at night.

▶ Dogs weighing 80 kilograms try to protect the herd against the wolves. According to the local people, the wolves are faster and cleverer in attack, even though the dog is a descendant of the wolf.

▶ These robust dogs never leave the herd. In an area where there are bears as well as wolves they are not a superfluous luxury.

PORTUGAL

AÇORES

AÇORES – ARCHIPELAGO

ENTHRALLED BY MOBY DICK

The Azores remind me immediately of two destinations which I visited extensively for my previous photography books: the mountains veiled in mist and the curtains of rain remind me of the Scottish Highlands, and the overpowering vegetation reminds me of the – almost vanished – rainforest of Madagascar. Man has impressed his ineradicable stamp on the Azores. I see meadows bordered with flowering hedges – all shades of green, outlined against a sea of blue. On some steep slopes you still find ecosystems that are completely intact, but it is not easy to walk there. The high level of humidity (80 per cent) and the rain keep intruders out. Sometimes I walk literally in the clouds and can't see my hand before my face. During a walk through the valleys – permeated with scents and filled with birdsong – I feel as if I am in a dream world. At night puffins sound like the screeching of a record that's worn to threads, or is it a cassette being rewound.

Around the islands there is a gigantic aquarium. But unfortunately every paradise has its devils. I dive among the dolphins in the open sea and suddenly feel an electric shock: I have encountered a jellyfish. For two days afterwards my face is on fire. Fortunately my eyes were protected.

I dive about 12 kilometres from the coast. Here all markers have disappeared. I am submerged in a world of blue, where dolphins circle around me and occasionally blow bubbles, only to disappear suddenly in the fathomless depths. I realize that the whales dive still deeper, in the clefts more than 2,000 metres below me. When they appear on the surface, the breath that escapes from their blowholes forms beautiful little rainbows. Birds install themselves on these temporary 'islands'. For a moment I see flashes of Jules Verne before me; the gigantic sperm whale is like Captain Nemo's submarine in *Twenty Thousand Leagues Under the Sea*. We spot a cow with its calf. The calf swims alongside and takes a moment to look at us with its strange, small eyes. Then it follows its mother to the depths. It is like encountering an extraterrestrial creature.

Whales

There are eighty kinds of whales in the world, twenty-one of which can be found in the waters around the Azores. Whalers used to range the ocean searching for a fountain of spray, which betrayed the presence of a sperm or fin whale. But firing off a harpoon has given way to the continual clicking of a camera.

Whaling developed between the eighteenth and the first half of the twentieth centuries. Whalers visited the islands from 1700 onwards and started a substantial whaling industry there.

Hunting for whales continued in the traditional way – with open boats and hand-thrown harpoons – until 1985. It is now prohibited.

Before the great oil boom the world turned on whale products: streetlamps worked on whale oil, children swallowed whale oil for their health . . . Now we no longer hunt whales, but we look at them. Although whaling is forbidden, Japan, Norway and Iceland carry on regardless, allegedly 'for scientific ends'. Whales die of chemicals, they are driven off course as a result of sound pollution or they end up in the nets of fishermen. In addition their food sources have dwindled as a result of the oceans warming and commercial fishing.

Sperm whales

The Azores are known for the constant presence of sperm whales. They stay close to the islands all through the year, and enjoy the clean water and abundance of food. Sperm whales are by far the largest toothed whales; the males can weigh 44 tons and reach a length of 18 metres. They are easy to recognize by their oval heads and the triangular fin between head and tail. When they are feeding on their favourite prey, the great squid, they can dive 2,000 metres and stay under water for an hour.

The last true wilderness

The author Philip Hoare is passionate about whales. The creatures intrigue him to such a degree that for four years he travelled round the world studying the complex relationship between men and whales. He wrote down his experiences in his impressive book Leviathan: or The Whale. Hoare calls the ocean 'the last true wilderness'. He tells us about his encounter with a sperm whale during a swimming party around the Azores. Beside the giant he felt insignificant: 'I had a feeling of infinity, of timelessness.' Whales can reach a lifespan of more than 100 years, they are intelligent and they continue to amaze us. For Philip Hoare the whale shows a kind of purity we have lost. 'It felt as if there had never been people, as if the ocean had become a Garden of Eden.' He praises the elegance and the freedom of the whale, freed from terrestrial gravity. 'The sperm whale is the largest beast of prey,' he says. 'It was terrifying until I felt his echolocation working. I felt a tremor right into my ribs. He scanned me and knew exactly where I was. Then he swam away. Amazing! I have never been so scared in my life. In the past I had considered whale-spotting rather pragmatically and objectively. But among the whales a feeling of guilt crept over me. As if I had to justify myself for the way in which we treat them. Whales are victims. But we live in enlightened times. I still hope that all this will change in the best sense!'

The Azores

The Azores (known in Portuguese as Açores) form an archipelago in the Atlantic Ocean at a distance of 1,448 kilometres from the Iberian peninsula and about 2,000 kilometres from the American continent. The archipelago consists of nine inhabited islands. Together they form – like Madeira – an autonomous region within the republic of Portugal. The Azores have a total land area of 2,247 km² and a population of about 250,000.

The nine islands of the Azores are all of volcanic origin and therefore rich in craters covered in lush vegetation, with deep and clear crater lakes and hot-water springs. The highest volcano is the Pico, on the island of the same name, which is 2,351 metres high, making it the highest peak in the whole of Portugal. The most westerly islands, Flores and Corvo, are some 500 kilometres away from the most south-easterly, Santa Maria. The Azores have a constant climate all through the year, with little change in temperature, which varies between 14°C and 24.8°C, with August being the warmest month. The seawater varies in temperature between 16°C and 22°C, under the influence of the Gulf Stream.

INTERVIEW WITH CONSERVATIONIST RUI PRIETO, OF THE DEPARTMENT OF OCEANOGRAPHY, UNIVERSITY OF THE AZORES

Which kinds of whales do we find near the Azores? Why?

You will find whales as well as dolphins here. It is not easy to explain why there should be so many different kinds in the same area, since every kind makes different demands on the environment. A number of aspects affect several kinds, so contributing to the exceptionally rich whale population of the Azores. Along the coastline of the continents there is a platform reaching several kilometres into the sea and which is on average 200 metres deep. This platform – the continental shelf – is characterized by its shallowness. This prevents large sea mammals from reaching the coast. Islands in the ocean, such as the Azores, are actually mountains rising from the bottom of the sea and breaking through the water level. There are also submarine mountains around the islands. This kind of island is not screened by a continental shelf, so a deep-sea (pelagic) environment develops around them. The ocean floor is very deep (a minimum of 1,000 metres), and you will find completely different kinds of creatures there to those in the shallow sea around the continental shelf. On the other hand the islands and the mountains under the sea in the middle of the ocean form a series of oceanographic processes which stimulate reproduction and attract predators. Moreover, the coasts of the islands form a substratum for algae and invertebrates, and offer protection to all kinds of organisms in sheltered bays and crevices between the rocks.

Some kinds of whales in the Azores – such as sperm whales – are rarely seen near the coast, because they look for their food at a great depth. They feed on squid and various kinds of fish and they need deep water to survive. The presence of islands and the submarine mountains may well encourage the populations living at great depths and create special circumstances which attract these animals. The islands may also offer protection in bad weather and form a shelter for young animals. Other kinds, such as dolphins, hunt near the islands and the submerged mountains as a consequence of the growth of local populations. Some varieties live near the islands throughout the year. Others spend only spring and summer there, when there is more food to be found. This may apply to the Atlantic spotted dolphin. Some migratory species – baleen whales (blue whales, common finback, Norwegian finback, humpback whales) – pass briefly by the islands during their trek to their summer feeding grounds. Researchers from the Oceanographic Department of the university of the Azores analyse why the Azores are so important for migrating whales with the help of satellite telemetry and photo-identification techniques. For some kinds, such as the Norwegian finback, the Azores may be a beacon on the way to the feeding grounds. For others, such as the blue whale and the common finback, the archipelago may have a role to play in their feeding habits. They stay in the area during spring for anything from a few days to a few months.

How many kinds of cetaceans are there in the area?

There are no recent data about the number of cetaceans that have been spotted around the Azores.

What are the most important threats to them?

There is hardly any industry in the Azores, and consequently pollution and accelerated destruction of the cetaceans' habitat are not a great risk. Nor do the nets used for fishing form a great risk. Monitoring reveals that there are few victims among the cetaceans and that there is little additional catch. Increased tourism and shipping can have an influence on cetaceans, partly from excessive noise and discharges. Even so, shipping movements in the Azores are still modest compared to those of other regions. Although the cetaceans there enjoy a relatively good environment, those seen around the archipelago can become victims of threats encountered elsewhere in the ocean, such as pollution by chemicals, noise pollution, degradation of their habitat, interaction with fishermen and climatic warming. Migrating cetaceans after all travel hundreds to thousands of kilometres every year.

What future do you see for these cetaceans?

The cetaceans are part of a complex ecosystem that is hard to understand and to control. Only with a better insight into that ecosystem and the specific role of each component of it will we succeed in managing the ocean in the long run. The future of the cetaceans and of all sea life is determined by insight into the processes of the marine life environment.

▲　The overwhelming growth of vegetation on some of the islands resulted from the high level of moisture and the prevailing air pressure. The inaccessible mountain flanks remain unspoilt.

▲　Here on the western boundary of Europe the lava creates spectacular shapes.

▶　A young sperm whale, keeping close to its mother, turns on its side to have a look at the world from the water.

▶▶　Dolphins race, jump and leap in the air. The Azores are a unique maritime inheritance, which need to be protected against industrial fisheries.

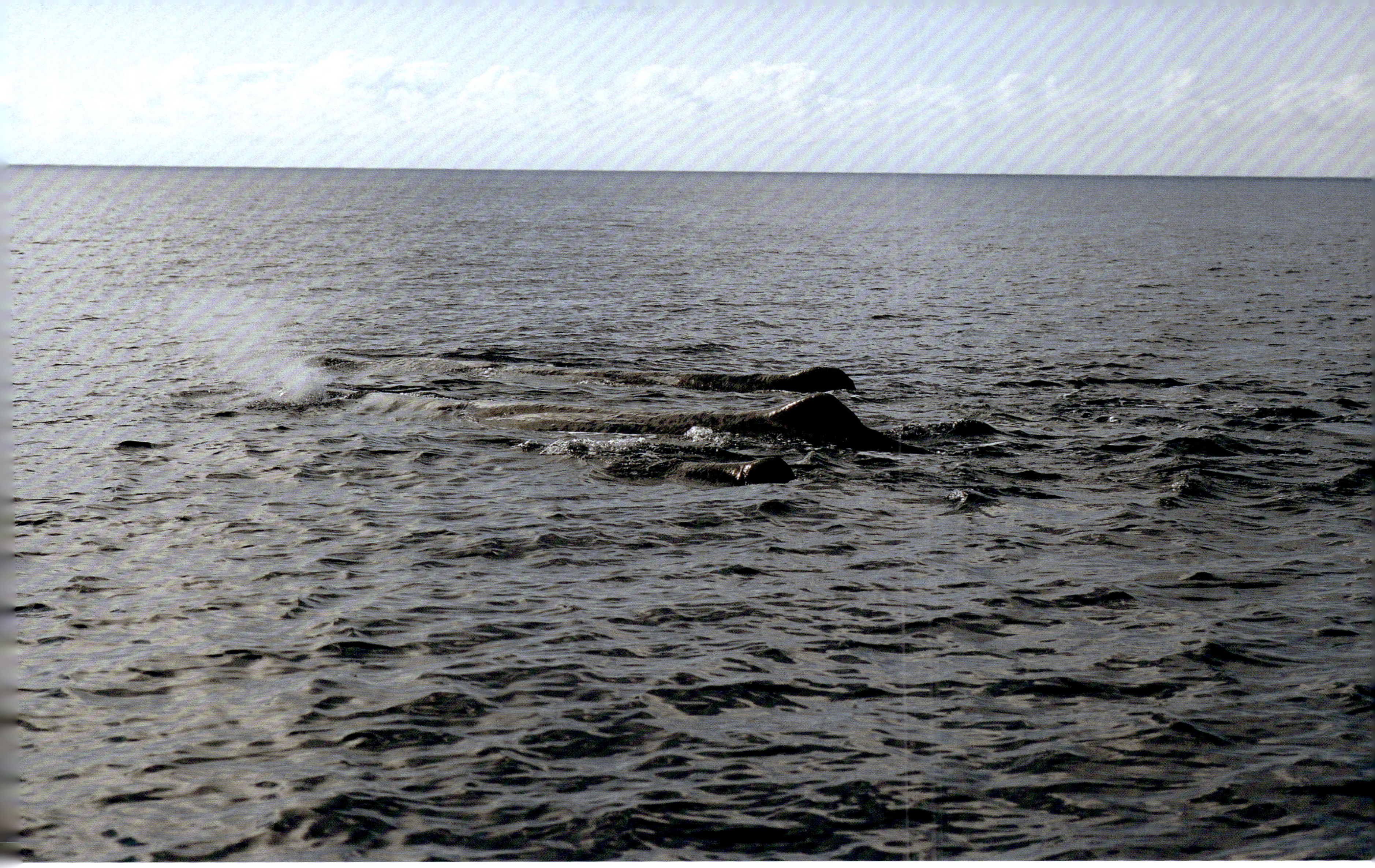

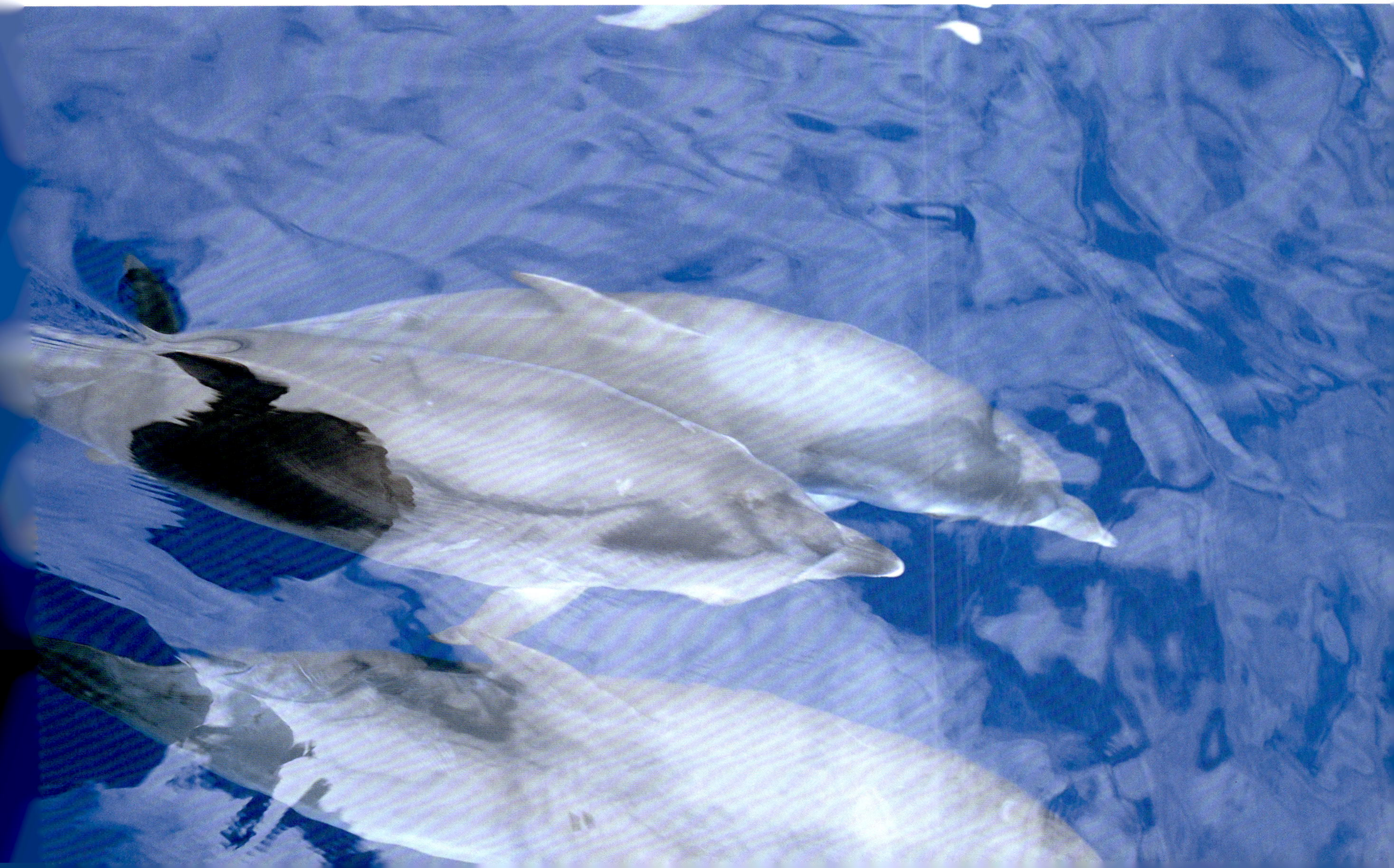

◄ The ground is spongy here and walking takes a lot of effort.

▲ A real microjungle, covered by various kinds of moss.

◄ Extinct volcanoes. Wild hydrangeas add colour to this green oasis. The view over the Azores keeps disappearing in thick veils of mist.

▶ Terns. Everything breathes softness in this area.

▶ Puffins. Their cries during their night flights sound like a tape being rewound.

▼ The undergrowth is a wonderland. Alice would feel at home here . . . Was Lewis Carroll ever here? Darwin certainly was!

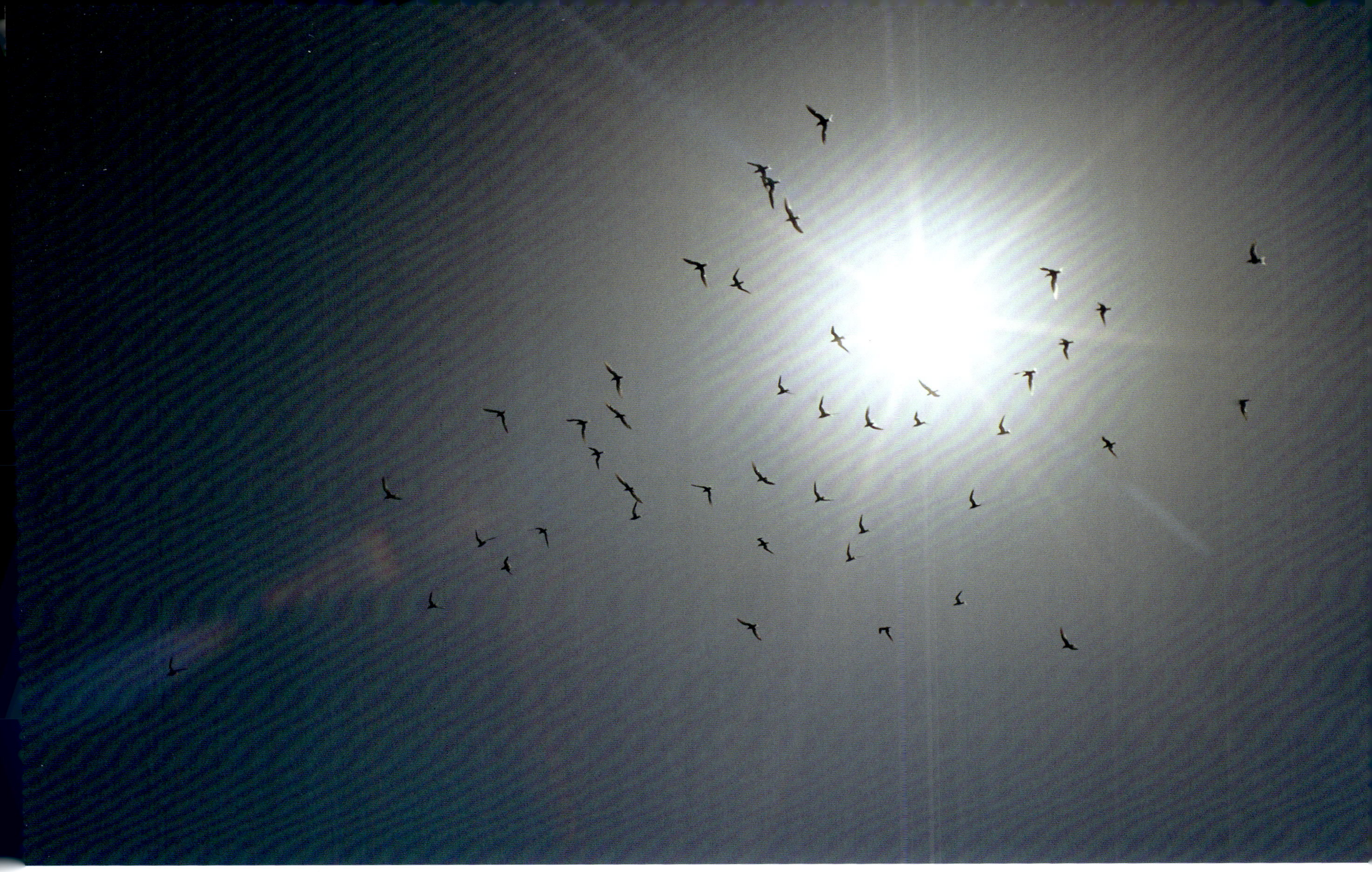

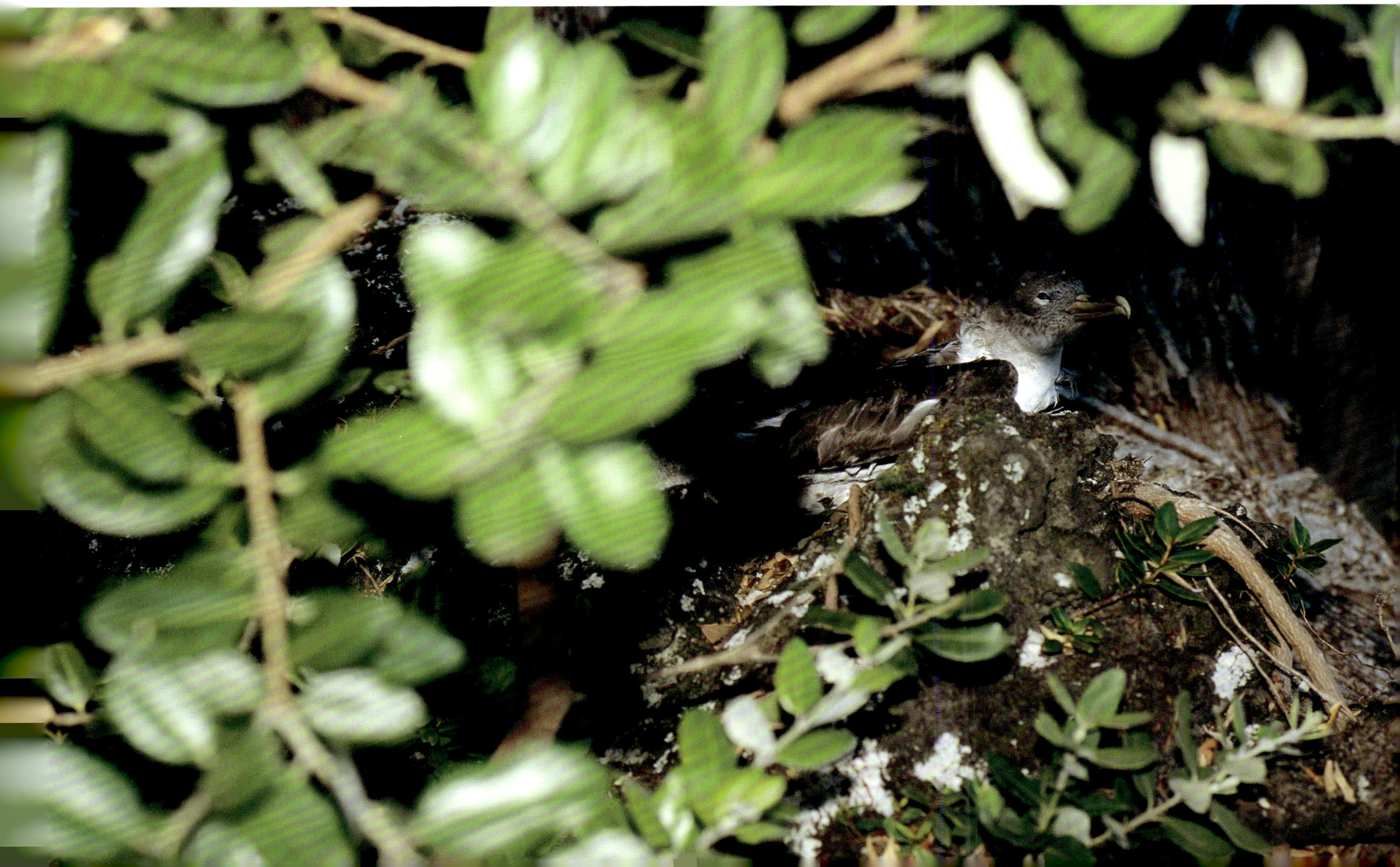

SUOMI

LAPLAND

LAPLAND – TAIGA

Tracks in the snow

When I look from the air at the desert of snow in the north of Finland, scenes from the film *Solaris* come to mind. This is Lapland at a temperature of –30°C. 'Keep moving' is the message in this country of wolverines, wolves, bears, elk, reindeer, eagles and otters. After a five-hour non-stop ride on a snowmobile I can feel my arms growing numb. Slowly the cold climbs up my back, like a clammy travelling companion. Although I am properly muffled up, no outfit can withstand these kinds of temperature with a headwind as well. Some animals deal with it more cleverly. Martens, for instance, dig tunnels 100 to 200 metres long under the snow, in order to move around.

I recognize the tracks of a wolverine, but I don't get to see one. This is not surprising, since even the director of the Kekkonen park knows this animal only from hearsay. A capercaillie decides to leave its hiding place under the snow. It sticks its head up, flaps its wings and takes flight. The noise of the snowmobile had woken it. I start looking for the wolverine, the spirit of the forest. A ranger tells me he has seen one. He tells me how shy and cunning the wolverine is, how it gallops and how hard it is to catch it on camera – even more difficult than the lynx.

I am riding through one of the largest areas of natural beauty in Europe, through a white desert, across bumps and between conifers. The snow muffles every sound in this silent world. At night, when the light of the moon and the stars is reflected in the snow, the landscape turns silver-grey. I can see flashes of blue and rose in the sky, but not yet the true Northern Lights. Together with the rangers, I follow the elk. From time to time we see them in the distance, dashing at high speed through the snow. There is something unreal about the experience. We take care not to exhaust the animals; in the middle of winter it is important to use as little energy as possible. Food is scarce and it is so cold that everything freezes in the blink of an eye.

We pass rivers where freshwater mussels show how pure the water is. Suddenly a ptarmigan flies up. A little further on we see tracks in several directions. They are all signs of life, but we don't get to see the life itself. It is hard in these parts. Success-ful sightings are scarce in these temperatures. I am travelling through a ghostly landscape. The trees, laden with snow, take on the most peculiar shapes. The wind blows the snow up into giant balls, which leave a track in a sea of white. Time and again the elk are too fast for us, and they escape across a hill or into the trees. The rangers tell me that the eagle hunts the elk, and that it pierces the lungs of its prey with its sharp beak.

We carry on looking for elk. Again they pop up in the distance. They flee with great leaps, on their tall legs, like dromedaries in a white desert, indefatigable. I discover an imperial eagle's nest.

We find ourselves close to the Russian border, where the wilderness just carries on. Wolves regularly migrate here from the east.

Kekkonen

The Urho Kekkonen National Park (2,550 km^2) in the far north of Finnish Lapland is protected by the Wilderness Act and is part of Finland's Natura 2000 network. The so-called 'wilderness' zones were started with an eye to sustainable environmental management and protection of the wilderness. The Finnish wilderness zones were set up in 1991 and together cover an area of almost 15,000 km^2. Kekkonen comes under the municipalities of Savukoski and Inari in Finnish Lapland. The park was founded in 1953 and stretches from the region of Tautatunturi in the north to the Savukoski forests in the south. In the east it borders Russia. The E75 road forms part of the western boundary. The 179-km^2 Sompio nature reserve lies within the boundaries of Kekkonen.

Rocks alternate with gently sloping plateaux, pine trees, mossy spruces, gloomy peat moors and meandering rivers. The environment is very varied and there are few differences in altitude. The river Suomujoki has left numerous lakes between the impressive forests. Next to the woods there is a sloping chain of dozens of bare, treeless, rocky hills. Gorges are covered with coniferous trees and lichen.

The Urho Kekkonen National Park is the natural biotope of bears, wolverines and wolves, which migrate from Russia. The golden eagle and the otter are permanent inhabitants of the park. Sami nomads also live in the area. They look after reindeer, hunt and fish. Traps, fencing for the herds, shepherds' huts and renovated settlements indicate their presence. Today, herding reindeer is still their main source of income in the area. Every now and then I see wild – or half-wild – reindeer, with or without their Sami herdsmen. The nomads live on the proceeds of their herd. The Sami protect the young reindeer from predators. They live alone in their tents, quiet and introverted, as I imagine mankind in its natural state to live.

Lemmenjoki

Lemmenjoki (2,850 km^2) in the north of Finmark – Finnish Lapland – is the most spectacular national park of Finland and one of the largest protected areas of natural beauty in Europe, with the most extensive uninhabited zone without roads. The Lemmenjoki National Park borders on the Norwegian Övre Anarjokka National Park. Large rivers alternate with forest, marsh and heathland. Extensive birch woods grow on the highest hills and along the edge of the bare peaks. The northern boundary of the spruce woods lies in the

▼ After my odyssey through Europe I conclude that the Finns and Russians have by far the best resistance to all weather conditions.

ecosystem?

Tapio Tynys: The volume of lichen is noticeably reduced in comparison with an area in its natural state. In the summer the grazing reindeer limit the regeneration of the birches, because they feed on the growing shoots.

Do the reindeer have natural enemies? Are there any large predators, and if so how many?

Tapio Tynys: Their natural enemies are wolverines, bears (except in winter) and golden eagles; also lynx, but to a lesser extent. As far as I know there are no permanent wolf populations, only occasional visitors. Obviously the predators have an impact on the reindeer. If you ask the reindeers' owners, they usually say that there are too many predators. It is generally accepted that the predators have their home in the park. But what is the ideal number and how do the herdsmen get compensated for animals that are killed? For the golden eagle compensation is based on the size of the population, and that system works well. For wolverines and similar animals compensation is calculated on the basis of the number of carcasses and the estimated number of carcasses.

Can you tell us something about the influence of the cyclic lemming population on the number of predators?

Tapio Tynys: The lemming population doesn't seem to be as cyclic as it used to be. I don't know how that came about. The cycle of lemmings and voles has a large influence mainly on small predators such as the stoat and on predatory birds such as the snowy owl and the rough-legged buzzard.

What are your views on the future for Lemmenjoki?

Tapio Tynys: Prospecting for gold is the most important activity in the park. It started in 1946, when the park was founded. There is a great debate going on about whether or not digging machinery should be banned when searching for gold. I think that looking for gold is an activity that is part of life in this area, and should be so on condition that it is done in the right way. People are interested in the lifestyle of the gold prospectors. But conservationists think of it as a threat, even if it takes place in a fairly small zone. Also, the number of reindeer is too large in relation to the available pasture. Keeping reindeer makes up part of life in the park too, but we argue for sustainable – rather than intensive – husbandry.

southern part of the park. The brown bear and the golden eagle are regular visitors. There is also a large elk population.

CONVERSATION WITH CONSERVATOR TAPIO TYNYS, OF LEMMENJOKI

Is Lemmenjoki important from the ecological point of view?

Tapio Tynys: Look at the surface area, the sub-arctic vegetation, the large, virgin forest and mountain zones, the mountain streams and rivers, the large mining areas: the Lemmenjoki valley is beautiful and very diverse, with a chain of rivers and lakes, coniferous forests and an exceptionally rich vegetation, and with deep canyons with steep walls. Together with the Övre Anarjokka National Park, Hammastunturi erämaa-alue and the Urho Kekkonen National Park, it forms a protected corridor from Russia to Norway, without roads and without permanent habitation.

How great is the impact of the large numbers of reindeer on the

▲   In the distance is Russian Karelia, a bit of Finland that was sacrificed to the Russians as a spoil of war.

▲   Every day I saw fresh tracks of the shy wolverine, but even the guides here have never actually seen one.

▲   Trees are covered with frost and snow. At a safe distance a capercaillie keeps an eye on us. Now and then one shoots out of his tunnel, like a jack-in-the-box.

▼   The elk moves about easily on the deep snow with his very large feet. His antlers can weigh as much as 35 kilograms. In Russian Karelia the elk is used for riding.

► Snowballs, chased by the wind.

►► Mussels survive only in very pure water and thus provide evidence of the quality of the living environment. According to scientists, these mussels live for two to three centuries.

▼ There are hardly any wild reindeer, my Sami guide tells me. The great migrations belong to the past. In deep snow the reindeer is sometimes prey for the imperial eagle.

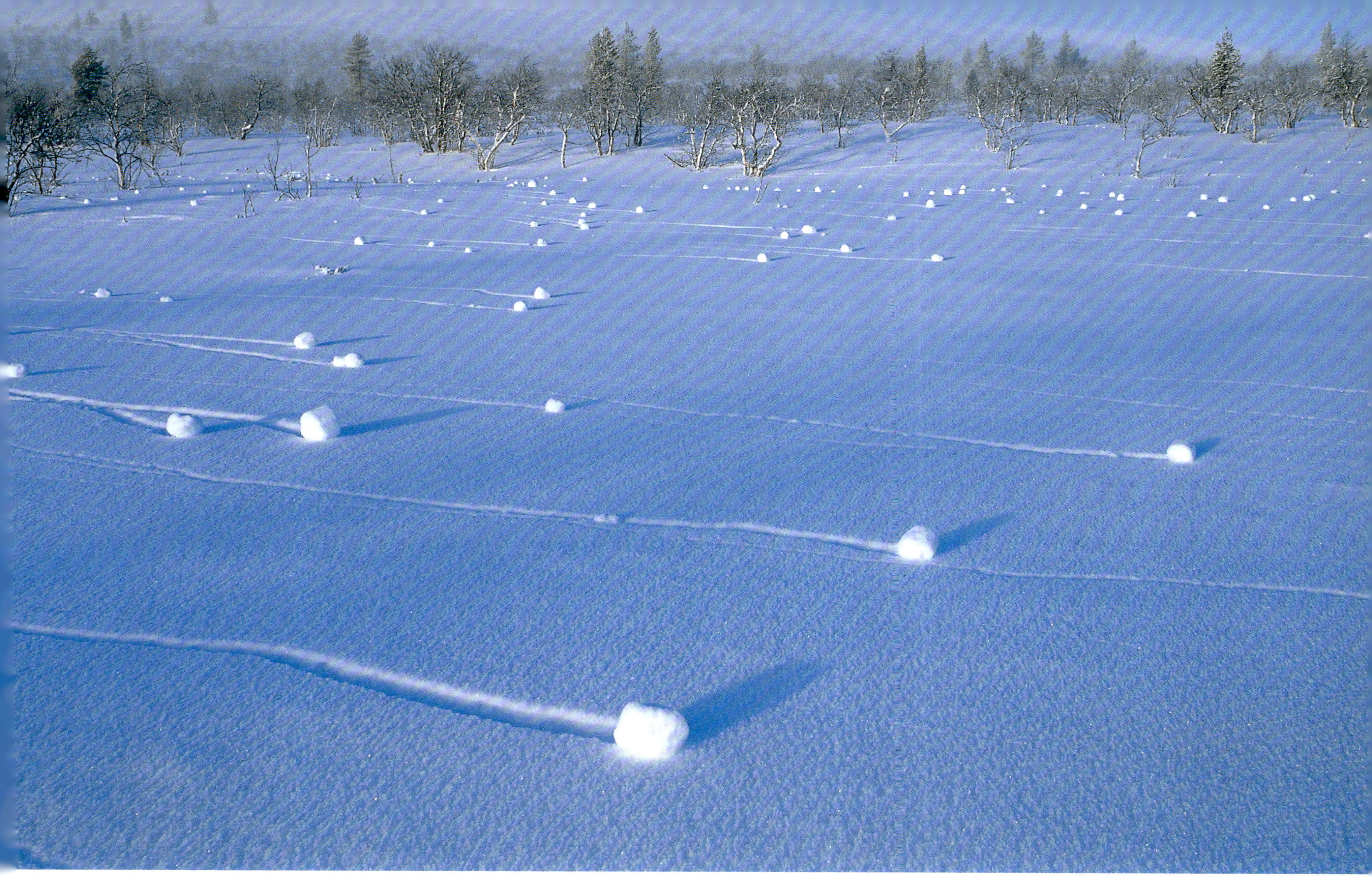

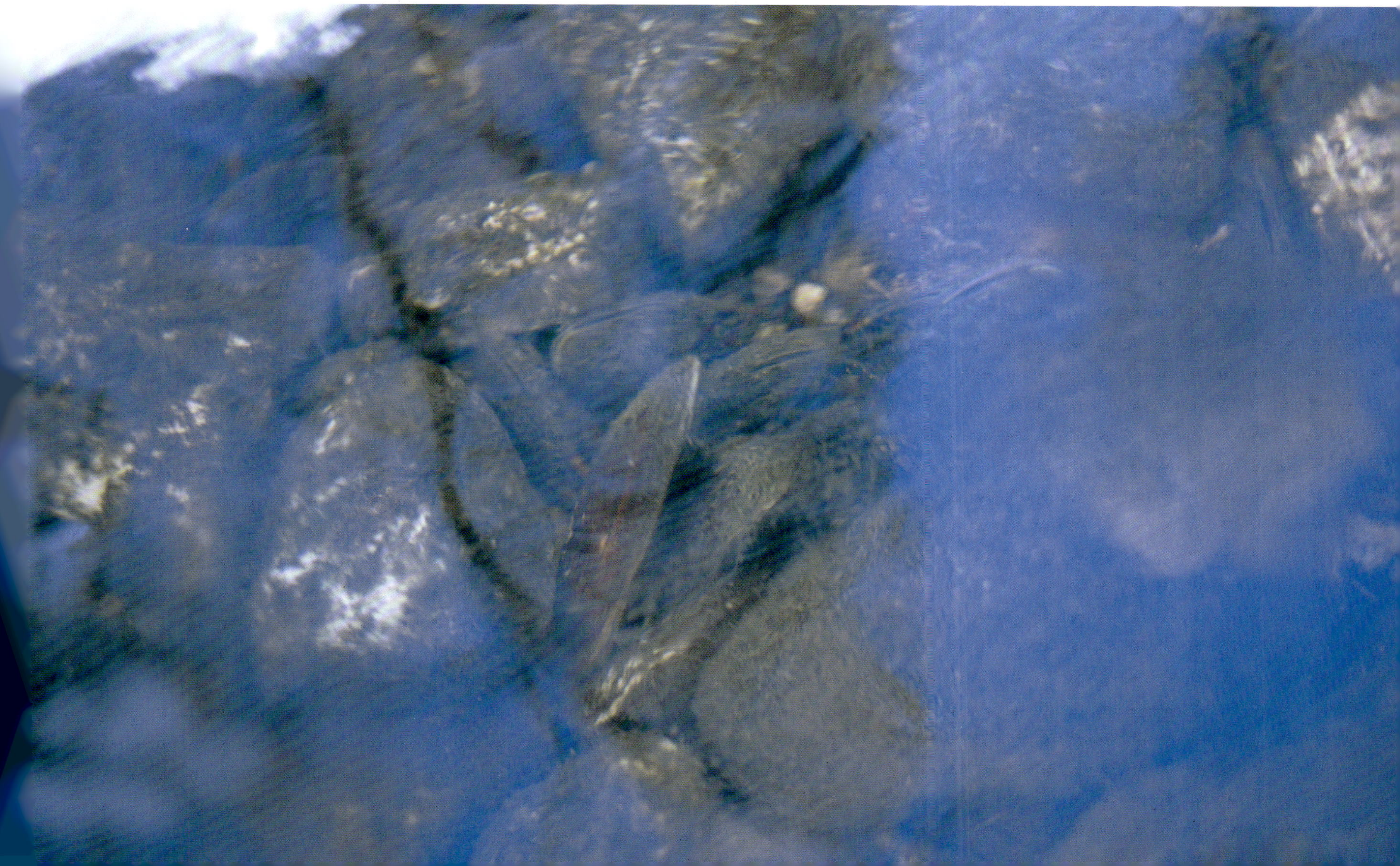

BASILICATA – ABRUZZO – ETNA

BASILICATA – HIGH WOODLAND AND DOLOMITIC ROCKS

THE BOSNIAN PINE DEFIES THE RAVAGES OF TIME

I can see an imperial eagle gliding past between the clouds. Its profile shows up beautifully in the lens of my binoculars. The remains of freshwater crabs are reminders of an otter's meal. Bosnian pines are the symbol of the park. The weathered, layers of bark make me think of the harness of a Roman soldier. There is the sudden hiss of a peregrine falcon skimming past. A couple meet high in the sky. I recognize a hawk by its silhouette. A peregrine chases a buzzard away. I watch a mass of black and red kites fighting against the wind. For three hours we walk along on snowshoes. The guide is afraid that he will get lost when the sky clouds over. The sirocco has covered the snow with a carpet of rosy sand from the Sahara. We walk through the remains of the high woodland, which is now regenerating. Here and there we can see traces of avalanches – a clear signal that we will have to take the iron laws of the mountains into account. The Soriano cat – neither a domestic cat nor a wildcat – has its permanent home in Basilicata. The griffon vulture has been newly introduced here. Some thirty individuals live in the park, but unfortunately we don't see any of them.

Pollino, 'the Dolomites of the south'

The Pollino National Park is the largest protected zone of the most recent parks in Italy. The tops (above 2,200 metres) of the Dolcedorme and the Cozzo del Pellegrino look out over the Tyrrhenian and the Ionian Seas. The park, established in 1993, stretches out over the southern Apennines. The mountains are the highest peaks in southern Italy and from November to May they are covered by a carpet of snow. The most beautiful area is made up of dolomitic rock, limestone cliffs, ravines, karst holes, very deep crevices of volcanic origin – so-called *timpe* – swallow holes, plateaux and alpine meadows. The zones covered with beech, chestnut and Turkish oak are populated by threatened animal species: the Apennine wolf, the Orsomarso red deer, the black woodpecker, the peregrine falcon, the eagle owl and the raven. In the highest zones you will find traces of the last Ice Age: the rare Bosnian pines, which owe their twisted shape to their never-ending battle against water, wind and ice. Small streams run down into the valley and fill the crevices of the Raganello, Lao and Rosa. Open spaces are taken up by cornfields, wild pear trees, brambles, hawthorn, holly, thistles, flowers, wild violets, orchids and peonies.

INTERVIEW WITH CONSERVATIONIST ESTER DEL BOVE, OF THE PARCO NAZIONALE DEL POLLINO

Can you tell me something about the history of Pollino?
The Parco Nazionale del Pollino (182,123 hectares) has harboured several population groups and cultures since the end of the Paleolithic era. This is clear from various archaeological sites, such as the prehistoric Grotta del Romito, one of the oldest and most important in Europe. Over the centuries the area has experienced the influence of the Greeks, Romans, Lombards, Byzantines, Saracens, Normans, Spaniards and the indigenous Lucani and Bruzi. An important testimony to this stirring history is the arbëreshe culture of the fifteenth and sixteenth centuries – the culture of an Albanian community fleeing from Turkish occupation. The memory of it still lingers today in certain traditions and clothing.

How important is the Bosnian pine, the symbol of the park?
An ecosystem evolved around the Bosnian pine. Various animals live in the centuries-old trees, among them the very rare jewel beetle. This beetle is a living fossil, possibly from the Tertiary period, easily recognizable by its golden or emerald-green colour with an azure-blue and purple sheen, 14–21 millimetres long. The species has adapted itself particularly to a cold climate and lives in the Mediterranean area at an altitude of up to 2,000 metres, mainly in old pines and conifers. The beetle generally stays hidden in the top of the trees. The larvae live in dead branches and stumps, where they feed on rotting wood. The jewel beetle can be found throughout the park, mainly in the Bosnian pine. A number of other species of beetle also attract attention: the Mediterranean stag beetle, the Capricorn beetle (Cerambyx heros), the Rosalia Alpina beetle and others.

What is the climate in Pollino?
The mountain range runs mainly in a north–south direction, with varying heights and differently oriented mountainsides. Because of the proximity of two seas there are a number of different climates, both on the side of the Tyrrhenian Sea and of the Ionian Sea. There is more rainfall on the lower height in the western part of the park. This is because of the dominant moist western wind, which is 'blocked' by the mountains, and because the temperatures in this part of the park are on average lower.

What is the relationship between the wildcat and the domestic cat?

From recent genetic research it appears that the European wildcat and the domestic cat belong to the same 'polymorphic' species and there are only subspecific differences between them. The wildcat avoids the higher zones because of snow, which makes it difficult for it to walk and hunt. It is a nocturnal animal. The number of wildcats is very limited, mainly as a result of the specific demands this species makes on its environment, such as the presence of vertebrate prey and its solitary and territorial behaviour. Its territory is actually very extensive, about 10 km^2. The most important threats to the existence of the species are the fragmented habitat, interference from domestic cats (bastardization, competition and transmission of diseases) and being hunted by the human race. It is very difficult to determine the degree of purity – and bastardization – of the population on the basis of morphological criteria. Up until now no research has been carried out in the park on the relation between the wildcat and the domestic cat.

What are the most important threats for Basilicata? What opportunities are there for the future?

The government and the general public will have to realize how important the preservation of the particular nature, history and culture of Basilicata is (specifically in the park). Furthermore it is of great importance that the volume of tourism is integrated in a strategy of sustainable management and that the initiatives are taken in the framework of a marketing policy based on ecotourism.

▲ *The imperial eagle. Like all birds of prey, it plays an essential role in the process of natural selection.*

▼ *The remains of an otter's prey, neatly laid out by a mountain stream.*

▼▼ *Centuries-old Bosnian pines stand like lonely beacons in this wild Japanese-style garden. During my ascent a peregrine skims past me to intimidate me, the turbulence causing a noise I shall never forget.*

▲ The European eagle owl is a superior bird of prey. When he establishes himself in a hunting area, he immediately cuts out all other predators.

▲▲ The wind forms veins in the snow.

▶ Mountain streams play an essential role.

ABRUZZO – HIGH MOUNTAINS WITH BEECH WOODS

AN EAGLE'S EYE ON THE ABRUZZI

It's pouring with rain in the Abruzzi. A troop of wild boar parades in front of me. When one comes uncomfortably close to me, I hide behind my camera. Intrigued, he comes closer, but then he slinks off again. Cranes circle high in the sky, their call ringing out like a trumpet. The tracks of wolves indicate rest periods during their migration. It starts to snow. A deer moves across the mountainside, its shadow outlined against the white; its silhouette looks almost demonic. I trudge along on snowshoes through a carpet of snow more than a metre deep. Suddenly I spot a group of four chamois, about 80 metres away. One of the chamois looks as if it is glued to the mountainside. A few seconds later an imperial eagle appears. The predatory bird has its eye on the chamois: a chamois means food for several weeks. The bird hopes to unbalance the animal so that it will fall down. I realize that this is an exceptional sight and count myself lucky that I can watch such a confrontation. There are, after all, only four breeding pairs of imperial eagles in the park.

Parco Abruzzo

The oldest national park in the Apennines is of essential importance for the preservation of the Marsican brown bear, the Abruzzi chamois and the wolf. Two-thirds of the area is covered with beech, making it one of the largest beech woods in the Apennines. The white-backed woodpecker lives in these large, old trees. The roe and the red deer have been reintroduced and wild boar have returned to this area. The food chain is now complete again, including the large predatory animals. The mountains form a changing and interesting landscape with peaks and steep slopes with an alpine character. The central zone of the park is watered by the Sangro river and its tributaries, and on the edge of the park flow the Giovenco, the Melfa and the Volturno rivers. The water often flows in underground channels and comes to the surface in the valley bottoms. There are two lakes in the park: the Barrea lake, an artificial lake fed by the Sangro, and the natural Vivo lake (at a height of 1,600 metres). The size of this last lake, which is fed by springs and melting snow, varies with the seasons. Above the valleys moraine depots, piles of stones, hollows, fractures and basins are testimony to erosion by glaciers and karst phenomena. In the park there is an abundance of limestone rocks. Near Camosciara the watertight dolomite rock ensures that the water can flow on the surface, where it forms waterfalls and basins. Animals are very shy in this environment.

The national park has around 2,000 plant species, including lichens, algae and fungi. The rare black pine may originate from the Tertiary period and can be found in certain zones of Camosciara and in the Fondillo valley. Among the conifers that grow naturally here you may find the mountain pines, which cover the vegetation zone between the beech wood and the alpine grassland, particularly in the Camosciara region. The predominant landscape, however, consists of beech woods, the natural vegetation of the Apennines for hundreds of years. The beech grows at an altitude of between 900 and 1,000 metres, covering more than 60 per cent of the surface area, and contributes to a colourful landscape which varies according to the season. The alpine grassland, which together with the meadows and open spaces takes up more than 30 per cent of the surface area, is typical for the higher mountain zones. Here the vegetation consists mainly of the yellow gentian, grass and cyperaceous grasses. The best-known flower is undoubtedly the Lady's Slipper, a yellow-black orchid, which grows in the heart of the reserve.

Bears and wolves

The Marsican brown bear, a subspecies of the brown bear, is the best-known occupant of the park. The bear, which can weigh up to 300 kilograms, is a quiet and solitary animal. This omnivore feeds on whatever its environment and the season have to offer: fruit, berries, grasses, insects, honey, plants, roots, carcasses and so on.

The bear lives in the woods and regularly visits the mountain meadows. It is not easy to observe it, but you should be able to find traces of its presence, such as the typical paw prints – clearly recognizable in the mud or snow – and upturned stones under which a bear has been looking for insects. The peaceful and tolerant Marsican brown bear succeeds in living among humans.

Another animal species, which admittedly is not only found in the park, is the wolf. One of the most hunted species, and threatened with extinction, it lives alone or in hierarchically organized packs. It is very energetic, skilful and wily, and is constantly on the move when in danger or when it is hunting. The wolf feeds mainly on small animals. It is not easy to observe. It is a nocturnal animal. In the daytime it hides in the wildest and most inaccessible places. Signs to indicate that you are in its territory are its droppings, which contain a great deal of hair, and its paw prints, which can be compared with those of a large dog but move in a single line.

INTERVIEW WITH CONSERVATIONIST LINA D'ORAZIO, OF PARCO ABRUZZO

Why do the Abruzzi form the 'wildest' region of Italy? What is the history of this region?
At the end of the nineteenth century only a few Marsican brown bears and Apennine chamois lived in the mountains. King Victor

Emanuel II had a royal hunting preserve laid out to protect the animals from extinction, but after a few years the hunting preserve was closed because of the high maintenance costs. On 2 October 1921 the so-called Pro-Montibus-et-Sylvis federation of Bologna, under the leadership of the botanist Romualdo Pirotta and the zoologist Alessandro Ghigi, promoted the foundation of the first protected zone in Italy. They borrowed 500 hectares of land from the municipality of Opi on the Camosciara hillside, the core of the current park, situated in the higher part of the Fondillo valley. On 25 November 1921 the autonomous establishment of the Abruzzo National Park became a reality. On 9 September 1922 the national park was inaugurated on the initiative of Erminio Sipari, a member of parliament. A zone of 12,000 hectares, extending over the municipalities of Opi, Bisegna, Civitella Alfedena, Gioia dei Marsi, Lecce nei Marsi, Pescasseroli and Villavallelonga, was designated and protected by law on 11 January 1923.

The Fondillo valley and Camosciara form the heart of the national park. In antiquity this area was inhabited by the Safini, the ancestors of the Samnites. Traces of these cultures can be found in the necropolis (of the seventh and sixth centuries BC) in the Sangro valley. The beech woods in this magnificent valley were cultivated until the Second World War. Since then the woods and the pure water of the Fondillo river have been protected. Now the valley has been saved and the old sawmill is being converted into a museum.

The Abruzzo, Lazio and Molise National Park is not only the oldest park in Italy but also the richest in terms of biodiversity. In the woods and on the limestone rocks live rare species of animals, such as the Marsican brown bear, the Abruzzi chamois, the Apennine wolf, the lynx, the red deer, the roe deer, the wild boar, the golden eagle and the rare white-backed woodpecker. There are more than 2,000 plant species, including the rare, beautiful lady's slipper orchid, the indigenous Marsican iris, the European trollius and the black pine of Villetta Barrea, which goes back to the Ice Age. Five of the twenty-five villages in the park are in the protected zone and are brilliant examples of the spontaneous architecture of the Apennines, their limestone, terracotta tiles and wooden beams seamlessly integrated into the landscape. The national park is a real cathedral to nature, which you visit with respect, without making loud noises and without bringing with you animals that might disturb the peace, without picking plants and flowers, without leaving litter behind and without straying from the signposted paths. If you walk along slowly and silently, with a little luck you may see a bellowing stag, a wild sow suckling her young, a roe deer in flight, a hunting Marsican bear or a wolf.

Why have the Abruzzi stayed so 'wild'? How has the area managed to escape the pressure of people?

The area owes its 'wild' character not only to government protection but also to its geographical location and the rather inaccessible mountains. Even the king found it difficult to come here and therefore rarely came to hunt. The Abruzzi are among the most sparsely populated areas in Italy. They are a green lung with three national parks, a regional park and more than thirty nature reserves.

How do you explain the presence of wolves and bears?

Populations of wolves, bears and chamois managed to keep going in this barely accessible area. Small numbers survived the Second World War and afterwards there was natural growth. Now the national park has 50 to 70 bears, 800 chamois and 60 wolves. The wolves do well because of the large number of grazing animals in this area, their favourite prey. The wolves have spread from the Abruzzi across the whole of Italy, and even into France.

Are the Marsican brown bear and the chamois of the Abruzzi indigenous subspecies and consequently unique in Europe?

The Marsican brown bear and the chamois of the Abruzzi are rare animals in the park and also all over the world. They are indigenous subspecies and that means that they are found only here. The scientific name of the Marsican bear is *Ursus arctos marsicanus*, so it is an acknowledged subspecies of the brown bear, which remained isolated. It is considerably smaller than the European brown bear and its coat is a light blond on the shoulders. The chamois is *Rupicapra pyrenaica ornata*. At one time there were only twenty left on a mountain in the park (Camosciara), but the population gradually recovered. Their way of life is adapted to the territory in the highest regions of the park. When there were sufficient animals in the park, the chamois were reintroduced successfully in other parks in the Abruzzi. This does not apply to the bear, which moves on every day and has a much more complex way of life. Possible reintroductions in other locations are much less obvious.

There are many species of deer and wild boar. Is this the result of a lack of predatory animals?

There were no wild boar in the park. They were introduced outside the park by hunters and eventually ended up inside it. Nor were there any deer left in the park: they were introduced in the 1970s. Now there are some 1,000 deer. Red deer, roe deer and wild boar are plentiful, but unlike in other regions of Italy the populations are controlled by the carnivores. For instance, 70 per cent of the excrement of wolves consists of the remains of wild boar.

What are your views on the future of this region?

It's not easy to foresee the future of this park. Everything is being done to maintain a unique and rare ecosystem. We can now claim to have ninety years of experience and are well placed to assess the threats and opportunities. For the last thirty years the park has played an increasingly more important role in the promotion of the natural environment. Every year we have about a million visitors here. Tourism is the most important source of income for the whole region. Obviously we promote a sustainable tourism which does not harm the natural sources. Sustainable tourism is the best way to make the public aware and keep them informed of the need for respect for the environment. In our view this is the only option for the future. Meanwhile we also subscribe to the European Charter for Sustainable Tourism and are working in close cooperation with the local tourist operatives. We are also continually working on the quality of the provision of services.

► The number of deer (of all kinds) has greatly increased since their reintroduction.

►► A local chamois. While I was here, an imperial eagle arrived and tried to frighten the chamois by flapping its wings. It wanted to drive him into the ravine. But the chamois reacted stoically and threatened the eagle with his horns.

▲ The endemic Marsican bear is smaller and lighter than the brown bear. Inbreeding threatens the survival of this subspecies.

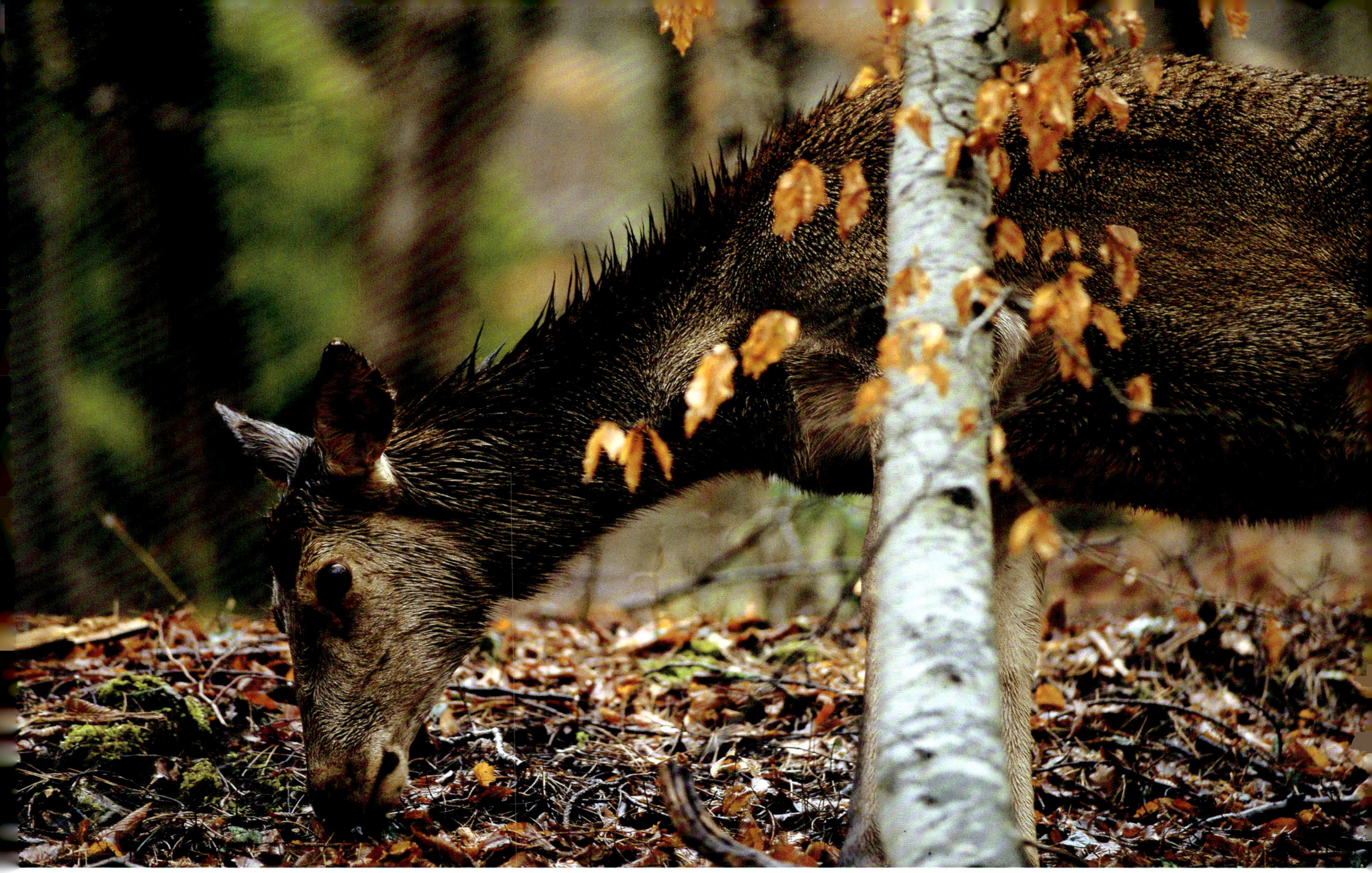

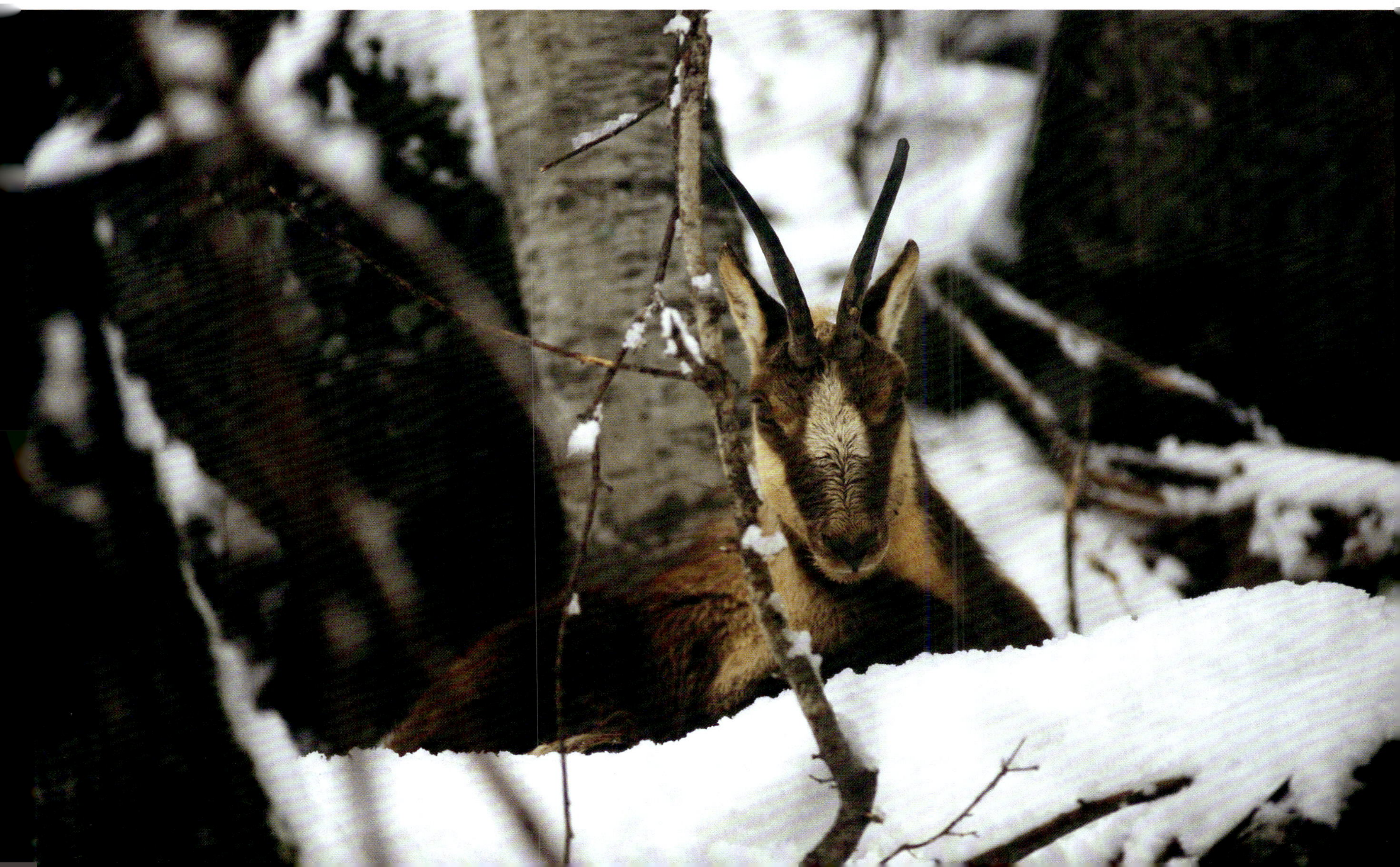

◄ *Valleys hide under clouds, mist, rain and fine snow.*

▲ *Cranes fly past, high in the sky. The birds will rest in the valleys for a week.*

▼ *An adult deer with imposing antlers searches for edible shrubs.*

ETNA – ACTIVE VOLCANO

STREAMS OF LAVA THROUGH THE WOOD

A lunar landscape around an active volcano in bright sunlight, outlined against an azure-blue sea. Once again it's like being in a story by Jules Verne. Round Mount Etna I follow the tracks of porcupines, martens and wildcats, but I don't get to see any of them. I catch a glimpse of a semi-wild boar, of the kind that sometimes crosses your path in Corsica.

After a few days it becomes clear why I find only tracks of wildlife: there is habitation everywhere – the houses have been built high against the sides of the volcano – and there is a great deal of hunting. The volcano cone is black against its blue background. Solidified streams of lava cut through the landscape, like four or five wide motorways. The sight is almost abstract and very graphic. The heart of the mountain is throbbing and from time to time I hear dull rumbles bubbling up from Europe's lower belly. The giant is alive. In 2002 molten rocks were vomited up from a depth of 20 kilometres. The woods have been destroyed by the lava. Dead white trees are lined up as if they are in a high-tech garden, sucked dry, aesthetic, like markings in a black valley.

After ten days I have seen only a pygmy owl. Walking across the solidified lava is not easy. I advance with difficulty between the brushwood where the wildcat may be hiding. I learn to judge the age of the lava by its colour. At intervals smoke escapes from a cavity in the Earth's crust. I can see the remains of fields of cactus, which in the past fringed the farmers' lands. The lava winds like a snake, hollow inside and armoured on the outside. A labyrinth of grottoes and caverns stretches for miles. An elegant, black ring snake leaves its trace. Is this the end of the world or its beginning?

Etna

Parco dell'Etna is amazing not only because of the volcano, the eruptions and the streams of lava, but also because of its exceptional nature, rich in sounds, scents and colours. The park extends from the peak of the volcano to the surrounding towns and is divided into four zones with varying degrees of protection. Parco dell'Etna was set up in March 1987. Etna is the highest volcano in Europe that is still active. Around it you can marvel at recent streams of lava next to older streams, in which larch, beech and birches thrive. In zone A (19,000 hectares) there is no human activity. This is the realm of the imperial eagle. Zone B (26,000 hectares) is built up with small fields and farms, barns and sheds indicate centuries of human activity. Zones C and D (14,000 hectares) are for tourist facilities.

Some 150 years ago Galvagni wrote about the wolves, wild boar and various species of deer – animals that have now vanished. The layout of new roads, deforestation and hunting threaten the survival of these and other species. Porcupines, foxes, wildcats, martens and rabbits populate the area, as well as weasels, hedgehogs, various species of mice and bats. There are many bird species, particularly birds of prey, in the untouched zones. Among the birds of prey that hunt by day are the sparrowhawk, the peregrine falcon, the kestrel, the buzzard and the imperial eagle. Among nocturnal birds are the barn owl, the eagle owl and the common owl. Herons, ducks and other wildfowl populate the Gurrida lake, the only lake near Etna. In the woods you may be able to glimpse a jay, a wood pigeon or a Greek partridge. In the highest zones around the lava fields the wheatear takes you by surprise with its fast, irregular style of flying. Various species of snakes, lizards and adders live here. Their numbers have increased in the absence of their natural foes. The insect world, too, is worth mentioning: butterflies, grasshoppers, crickets and bees play a crucial role in the ecological balance.

The flora is exceedingly rich and varied, and consequently the landscape changes continually. This is linked to a compact soil, to the continual changes in the substrata due to the rivers of lava, and to the rains at this altitude and on the outcrops. In the lower regions you can make out the holly-oak woods next to vineyards, hazel, species of oak, orchards and chestnuts. Above an altitude of 2,000 metres you will see beech woods. Next to the woods the landscape is marked by thorn bushes, which protect other mountain plants, such as violets. Past the boundary of thorn bushes, between 2,450 and 3,000 metres above sea level, few species are capable of withstanding the harsh environment of Etna.

Active volcano

In the east of Sicily the enormous bay that stretches from the Pelorian to the Iblei mountains became filled with submarine lava eruptions (from which Etna originated) and by the sedimentary deposits of the Simeto river. A deep depression of 7 by 7 kilometres formed on the east side of the volcano. The walls are 1,000 metres high. Most of Etna's lava flows are built up of fragmented materials with a rough surface. In rare cases the lava feels softer and smoother. The first eruptions took place half a million years ago. Some traces of the phenomenon can be found in Aci Castello, Aci Trezza and Ficarazzi. Mount Etna is locally also called the Mongibello, from the Italian word monte and the Arabian word jebel, both meaning 'mountain'. According to the Italian author Leonardo Sciascia, Etna looks like a 'large cat, which lies purring peacefully and every now and then wakes up for a while'.

Mount Etna is the highest mountain on the island and the highest volcano in Europe (3,350 metres). The highest accessible point is near the Osservatore at nearly 2,000 metres, situated in a bare 'moon landscape' where the smell of sulphur becomes noticeable. After Stromboli, Etna is the most active volcano in Europe and one of the most active in the world. The greatest eruption of the past century was in July 2001. The most recent ones happened in the night of 4–5 September 2007, on 23 November 2007 and on 10 May 2008. The worst eruptions were in 1381 and 1669, when the lava reached the town of Catania.

Wildcat

A number of factors explain the presence of the wildcat. In the first place there is the protection of the whole volcanic area. In addition there are various habitats at various altitudes, and finally also the rabbit population. Because of the human presence in the area the wildcats are mainly active at night. One of the factors disturbing the animals is the forestry operations. The lava flows provide good hiding places for the wildcats.

Lunar landscape

The unique landscape of Mount Etna resembles the landscape of the moon, with nothing but rocks. But because of the action of rain, ice and wind the lava flow makes an ideal soil for Mediterranean vegetation. On Etna there are two indigenous species of tree: the Etna birch and the Etna broom. Also important is the variety of habitats on Mount Etna. In the habitats on the higher levels, with only small plants, the biodiversity is limited, but the woods at lower altitudes provide good habitats for animals. The presence of the large populations of rabbits encourages the growth of the wildcat populations.
(Source: Stefano Anile, biologist, Parco dell'Etna)

▲ *A real witches' cauldron, much larger than I had ever imagined.*

▲ *Here you can feel the pulse of the earth. At intervals poisonous gases escape.*

▲   Animals turned to stone or sculptures? The
cooled lava forms a new crust.

▼ *The wildcat roams in an area around the volcano. Some decades ago there were still wolves.*

◄ A charred wood is evidence of the passage of a lava flow. The wood will come to life again within fifty year.

SRBIJA

DONAU

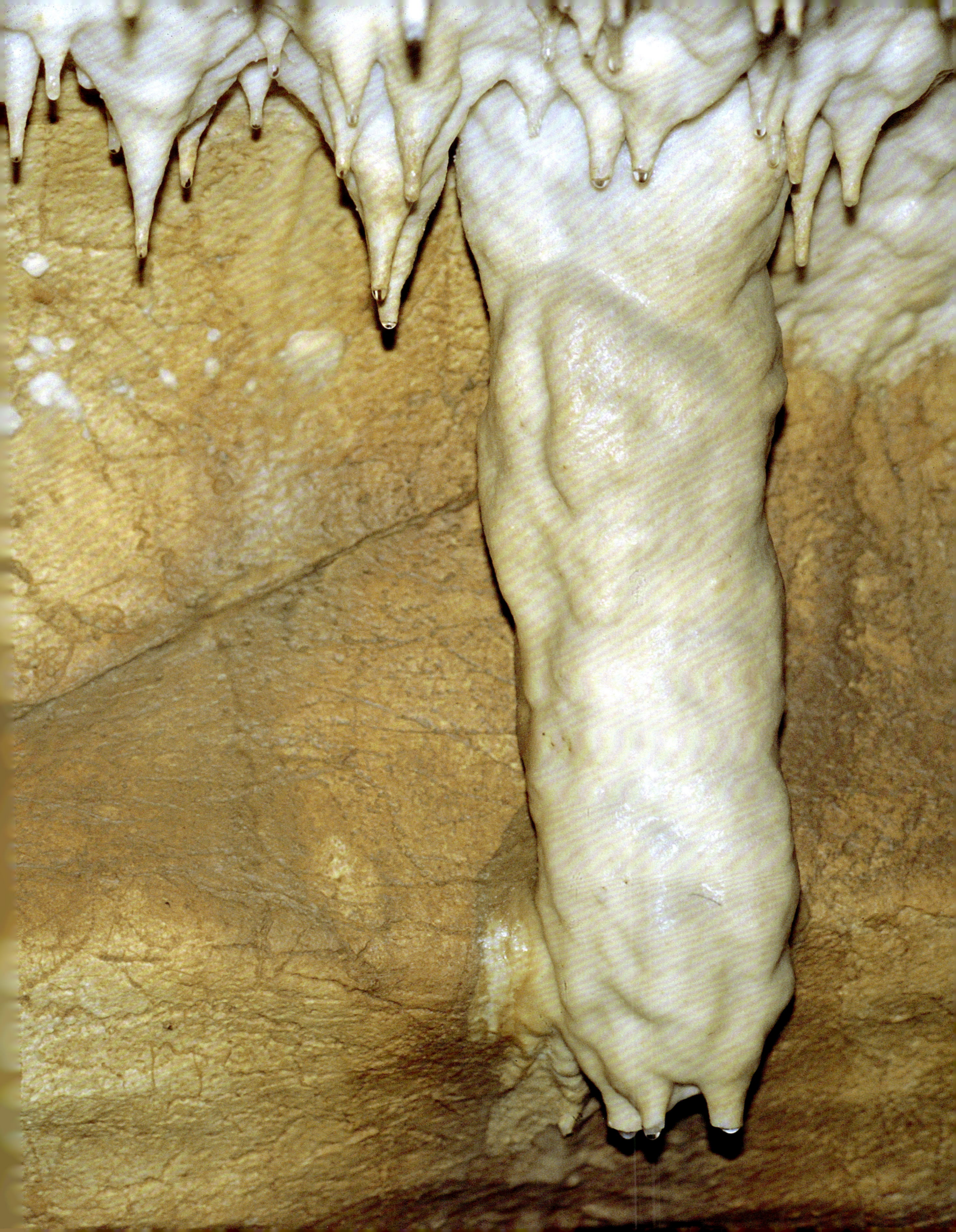

DONAU – GORGES AND RIVERBANK ZONES

THE HEART OF THE BALKANS

In some places the Danube is very wide, 6 to 8 kilometres. Otherwise the landscape does not look particularly exceptional to me. Together with the guide, I search for jackals, but all I see in front of my lens is a rabbit. According to the ornithologist on duty, 'Anything is possible here.' 'I'll show you an eagle's nest!', he promises. 'When did you see the eagles last?' I ask. 'Five or six years ago!'

On the other side of the valley, in Romania, I can hear liturgical songs. The atmosphere is indescribably magical. There is talk of wolves, but unfortunately they are too highly prized as a hunting trophy for a sighting to be likely. I see a little egret, looking for the fish that swim up the confluents to spawn. We enter the underground grottos of Rajko. These are populated by bats, hanging by their little claws and respectably covered by a cloak of wings. We walk for a kilometre and a little further on come to the playing field of the speleologists. The complex of grottoes is particularly beautiful, with magnificent galleries. And bats within hand reach.

Djerdap

The Djerdap park (64,000 hectares) is on the Danube – from Golubacki Grad to the dam in Sip – where Serbia borders on Romania. It's the heart of the Balkans. The most important identifying mark is the Djerdap gorge, known as the Iron Gate. The gorge extends over nearly 100 kilometres along the flanks of the Carpathians and forms the wide and deep Danube valley. Here is one of the deepest river passages in the world, with basins up to a depth of 82 metres. The gorge really consists of three gorges (Gornja Klisura, Gospodjin Vir, and Veliki and Mali Kazan) separated by ravines. Where the river narrows to 150 metres, in Kazan, the cliffs rise to a height of more than 300 metres. The Djerdap gorge was formed by the Danube, the second longest European river, which flows through eight countries (or forms the natural frontier between them). Djerdap is a typical river-valley park. The morphological diversity is encouraged by a large number of gorge-like valleys formed by confluents of the Danube, karst relief on limestone plateaux and other geological phenomena.

The Djerdap gorge is the longest fault line in Europe and is an exceptional natural phenomenon. Because of its sheltered position more than fifty woodland and shrub communities have survived. Some of them are the remains of earlier woods from the Tertiary period. The shrubbery forms only a limited part of the vegetation. In addition there are many grasses in the woods, in the meadows, on rocky terrain and on the rocks. The indigenous species are particularly important because of their specific ecology and sparse dissemination. In total more than 1,000 plant species are registered.

Worth mentioning are the Turkish filbert, the witch hazel (Hamamelis), the European nettle tree, the holly and the rustyback fern. Wild animal species include deer, roe deer, wild boar, badger, hare, chamois, fox, weasel, lynx, wolf, bear, marten, jackal, short-eared owl and black stork. The park is a migration stop for hundreds of thousands of migratory birds who reach their winter or summer habitat via the Djerdap gorge.

The river Danube is a suitable habitat for, among others, European catfish, sturgeon, perch, barbel, bream, pike and carp. Before the construction of a large dam there were 61 species of fish from 13 families. The construction of the dam influenced the fish stock by interrupting the routes to their spawning places. As a result the white sturgeon and the sturgeon from the Black Sea, among others, became rare. Now some Asian and American species have been introduced.

Because of the combination of the geographical location, the microclimate and biological, natural and historical factors, the Djerdap gorge is a unique refuge for wild animals in Europe. But man, too, has made use of the location and its natural protection. Archeological finds indicate a human presence as early as 7000 BC. Lepenski Vir was a centre for hunting, religion and art. The earliest monumental art works from central and eastern Europe are to be found there, as well as the oldest forms of organized communities in the Danube basin. Lepenski Vir is an impressive illustration of the link between man and nature, of the role and meaning of the natural environment for life and culture, with traces of Roman, medieval and Turkish civilizations. The Roman emperors Tiberius, Claudius, Domitian and Trajan built a strategic road, bridges and fortifications in the Djerdap gorge. The medieval fort of Golubackigrad guards the entrance to the gorge, and Fetislam dates to the Turkish occupation.

ROSSIJA

DONO & WOLGA – URAL

DONO & WOLGA – STEPPE

A BILLOWING SEA OF GRASS

An ocean of grass. Fascinating for its sea of space, unbounded. Interrupted only by the Volga, the Don and the marshes. Infinite, without riverbanks . . . Summer shimmers across the steppe, the heat pumping all life away. On the banks of the Don the wind rises. Between the waves of the grass flutter colourful bee-eaters. Dust blows high over the sandy roads. Ospreys float on the banks of the river.

This is the land of the Russian Borzoi. This great greyhound is used to hunt for jackal, fox or wolf. It is super-fast and has great endurance. It is the hunting leopard of the steppe, as fast as the wind. When a pack of these hounds spot a wolf they will go for it and surround it until the Cossack huntsman rides up and shoots or sabres the animal to death. I meet a real Cossack with a pack of Borzois. The dogs do the preparatory work. They hardly touch the ground as they run and seem to float. These hounds have been designed for the steppe and for pure speed. The end of this story is not hard to guess . . .

Insects proliferate in the grassy vegetation. It teems with hornets. The vegetation varies in kind and colour, from yellow to a bright orange. I experience a sense of infinity, a subtle beauty in a world without people, a world of empty plains and eroded hills, gentle and withered at the same time. The wind caresses the billowing heads of grass, which turn gold in the dying sun. I could never have imagined so many kinds of grass.

In the wild river Don enormous sandbanks have formed. The presence of masses of river crayfish show that the water is pure. I can see a great bustard. I spot a rare lanner falcon. To see the night come down across the steppe is quite an experience. On the horizon the light fades. Nature here seems inexhaustible.

Steppe

A steppe is a treeless landscape where only short grasses grow. Steppes occur in areas where there is a drought for eight to nine months a year and where no trees grow for lack of rain. When it rains, the yellowy grass suddenly turns green and herblike bushes come into flower.

The Russian author Chekhov sings the praises of the steppe in his story of the same name. It is high summer and during the long journey he sleeps at night on a hay cart. Lying on his back he listens to what the older people are talking about and gazes at the star-studded sky. Then he lets the conversation die, pulls out all the stops and brings the steppe to life:

▶ *The Borzoi greyhound belongs to the steppe, a survival from the time of the Tsars.*

Suddenly, straight above his head, the heavens broke into pieces with a terrible, earsplitting crack. He bowed down and held his breath, expecting the fragments to come down on the back of his head and on his back.

Anton Chekhov, *The Steppe*, 1888

▶ *The steppe is a sea of grass, dotted with an endless number of flower species. Every time you take a step, a cloud of colourful insects flies up.*

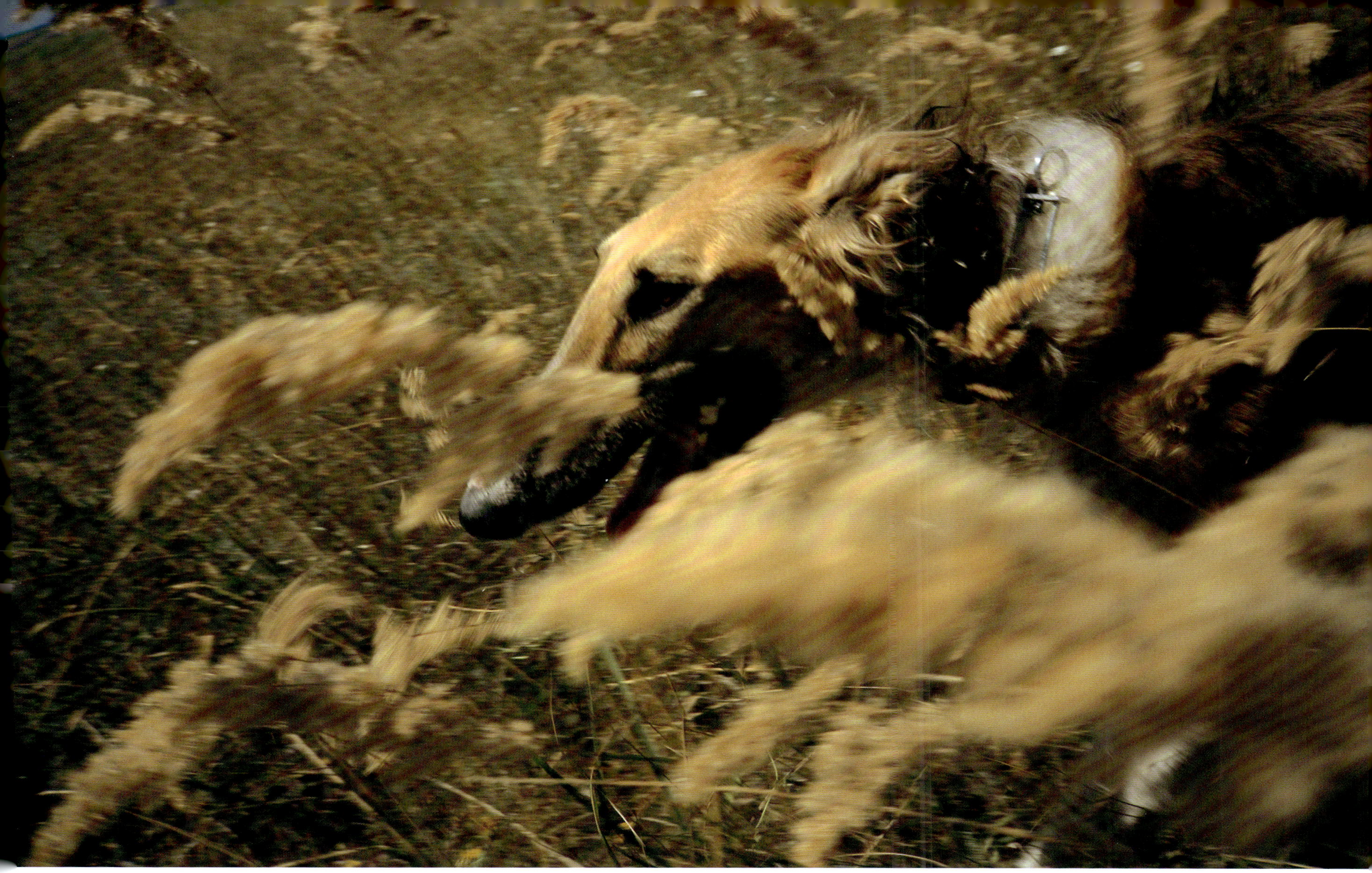

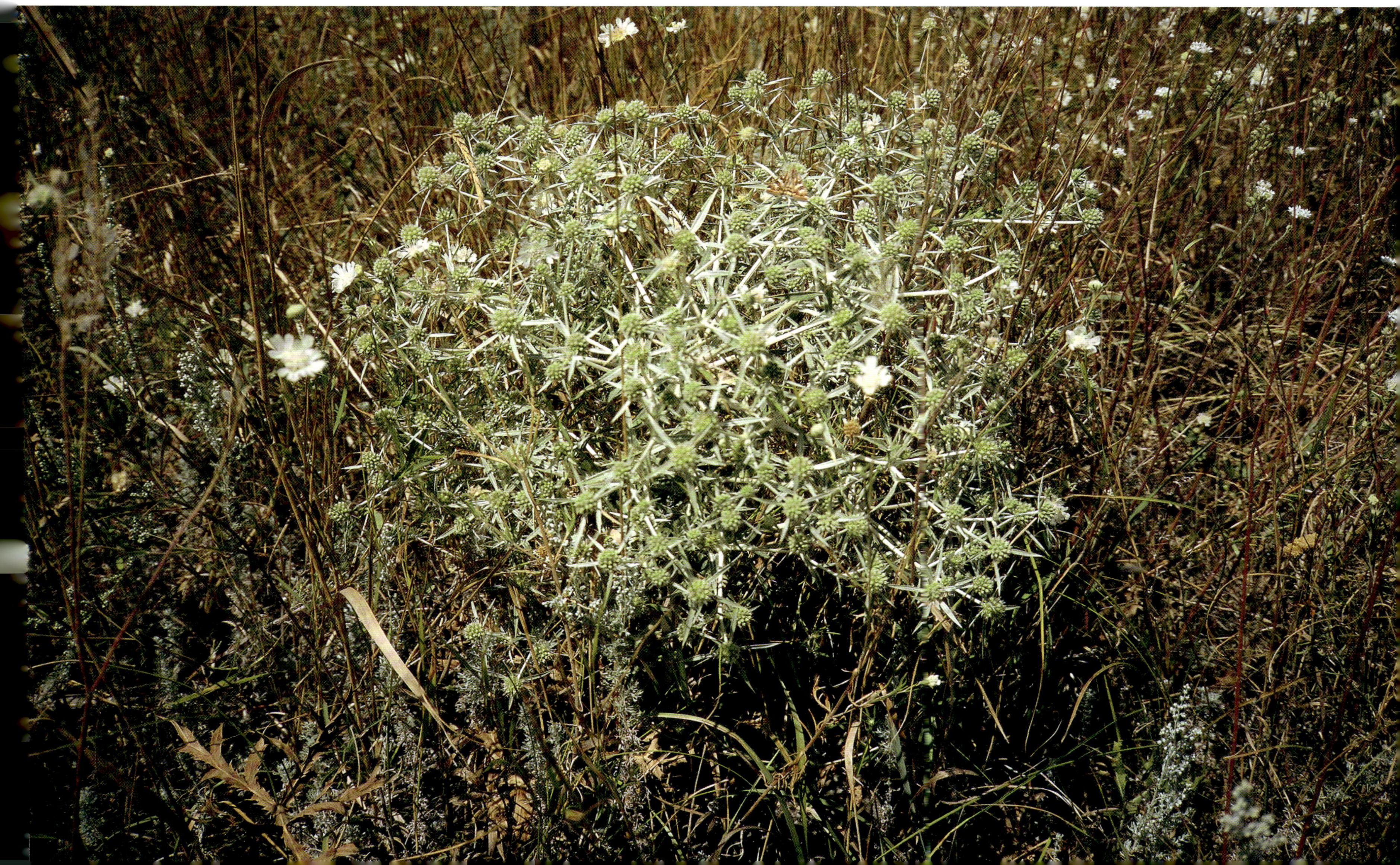

▲ In this continental climate the heat is exhausting. The few cattle are harassed by enormous badgers.

▲ Borzoi dogs are used to drive game. I saw a Cossack woman using them for the hunt – a picture straight from the novels of the great Russian writers, such as Turgenev, Arsenev or Chekhov.

A PLACE OF CONIFERS

In a village the carcass of a deer is hung up to attract bears, which have plundered the farm stock. I meet people with Asiatic features. All the houses are made of wood. I see flowers everywhere in an area that is known for the quality of its honey. The rivers are wild. Nature surprises with its subtle herbs and spices. Here the environment embraces civilization rather than the other way round. I leave the town and am immediately surrounded by nature. All predators – beasts and birds – are present here. Crowds of raven and hooded crows set up a cackling concert. I see some crows chasing away a light-coloured hawk. I hope I will be able to watch a bear, a wolverine or a badger. The landscape makes me think vaguely of the Vosges in France. The Urals are a very accessible mountain range, partly covered with a taiga of conifers, which alternates with extensive birch forests. Once more, coming from a small country, I am overwhelmed by the awe-inspiring amount of space on the edges of the European continent. Is this in fact still Europe?

Ural

Baskiria is in the south of the Ural mountains, which are more than 2,000 kilometres long and 300 kilometres wide, with peaks 1,000 to 1,500 metres high. The Urals run roughly from north to south and form a boundary between Europe and Asia on the Eurasian continent. This is the longest mountain range in Europe. The highest peak, at 1,894 metres, is the Narodnaya (People's Mountain) in the north. The Urals stretch from the steppes in the northern frontier zone of Kazakhstan to the coast of the Arctic Ocean. The northern extensions of the mountain range are the island of Vaygach and the island group of Nova Zembla in the Arctic Ocean.

INTERVIEW WITH ORNITHOLOGIST KAREV EVGUENY

What makes this area so exceptional ecologically?
We find ourselves on the boundary between Europe and Asia. The landscape consists of dark taiga of conifers, wide stretches of deciduous forest and steppes.

What birds do you find here?
Don't ask me to list them all! Riabitsev's *Birds of the Urals, pre-Urals and Western Siberia* mentions 430 species. Baskiria has more than 200 species..

Why are the birds larger and lighter in colour in the north and the east?
It is a recognized zoogeographic phenomenon among birds and mammals. In colder regions large animals have an advantage because with their larger body surface they suffer relatively less from the cold than smaller animals (the cold spreads itself over their body more). To answer the second part of your question, the farther you travel to the north or east, the more snow you meet. A white pelt or plumage consequently offers more protection.

◄ *The valleys of Baskiria in the Urals are 2,000 kilometres long, 300 kilometres wide. I followed in the footsteps of the writer Louis Aragon as far as the border with Siberia.*

► *The Eurasian lynx. In a remote hamlet I observed a young lynx playing with the ranger's cat. Perhaps the temporary adoption was a result of the death of the lynx's mother.*

▼ *The Urals are no higher than the Vosges in France, but much more mysterious.*

▲ The goshawk. In the north and east this bird is rather more corpulent.

▶ Young goshawks. Adult goshawks are ferocious birds of prey. Eat or be eaten!

▼ Domestic geese with their young. Although geese are good guards, they often fall prey to predators.

BELARUS

BEREZINA

BEREZINA – SWAMPS, PEAT AND RIVERS

CAUGHT IN THE SWAMPS

Napoleon had to break off his campaign here when he was driven back by Kutusov and his hordes of muzhiks. Of the 650,000 soldiers who crossed the Berezina, barely 30,000 came back. They were overtaken by the Russian winter. I discover fragments of shells and bones of partisans in flooded trenches. In this impenetrable swamp silence reigns, occasionally broken by the reports of a shotgun. I hide, in order to look out for an elk, but I don't get to see this large animal: I see only a small one, a little owl. This is the smallest European owl, no bigger than a starling, which looks like a small head with wings. A raccoon appears and disappears again. A hawk swoops on a henhouse; an eagle and a sparrowhawk circle high in the sky. A wolf slides from the bank into the river. A grass snake slips away. I am watching timeless tableaux. I install myself in the abandoned nest of a white-tailed eagle, 23 metres high, and enjoy the view across the swamp, with an elk in a far corner. In the villages the inhabitants fill wooden tubs with their winter stores.

At night I watch beavers. I study the tracks of wolves, elk and wild boar in the sand. The silence is deafening. Great crested grebes float on a golden lake. Meanwhile I am devoured by mosquitoes, here in the southern end of the taiga. Horseflies are 3 or 4 centimetres long. Man is not welcome here . . . A black woodpecker knocks at a steady rhythm. I spot a rare night swallow. The droppings of a bear give me a glimpse of his last meal: ants. This is pure nature. Every link of the ecosystem works. In the village children romp around with a stork. A young lynx hides itself under a seat in a living room. It is playing with a house cat and looks a great deal more agile. Young black storks try to hide in their nest. I wait while hundreds of mosquitoes carry out an uninterrupted attack. I wait in the pouring rain. And then I see a wolf. What at first looked like a hare turns out to be a wolf cub. It scans me for an instant, and then takes to its heels, at a rate of knots. At the same time I see an adult animal urinating and through my binoculars I catch sight of a pack of about ten wolves.

Walking here is a laborious progress across tree trunks. Conifers survive for a 100 to 140 years, until a storm destroys them. Under a blanket of green a large carpet of moss and lichen has formed. Something moves 40 to 50 metres in front of me. A wild boar? An elk? The wood is so dense that I can't see it. An adder hisses threateningly in my direction when I surprise it. I walk through a battlefield of fallen trees, between beavers' dams. Nature is in chaos here. A capercaillie rises, its wings flapping. Then I find myself confronting a young wild boar. Perhaps the animal came from the mass of blueberries stretching out in front of me. Everything is possible here. From a canoe I see a lesser spotted eagle gliding under a beautiful layer of clouds.

A capercaillie, the head of a beaver cleaving the water, an osprey . . . The upstream journey on the Berezina river recalls the atmosphere of Apocalypse Now, accompanied by a choir of frogs and a flight of dragonflies. I feel as though I have found paradise in the far east of Europe. I move from one timeless scene to another, exchanging one unforgettable emotion for another.

Downstream I let myself float along on the gentle current. Two nightjars are born right in front of my eyes. Swarms of butterflies and storks surround me. I detect the rare greater spotted eagle. In the morning the woods sing with the voice of the golden oriole. Here everything in nature is as it should be. The storks are as plentiful as the swallows. This is how the woods in the Ardennes used to be a thousand years ago, I think to myself. While swimming in the river I am accompanied by geese. This voyage of discovery in the heart of the European primeval forest will stay in my memory for ever. In the background the long, muted cries of the elk resound. I find myself in a labyrinth of woodland in which it is easy to get lost. The Belorussian rangers say: 'I've got a good trip for you!' Which is as if to say: 'Puzzle it out for yourself!' Vladimir challenges the wolves with a blood-curdling howl. A wolf, 1 or 2 kilometres away, answers him. It is amazing how man and beast can understand each other.

Berezina

In the Belorussian countryside the modern world is absent. The farmers live in traditional, wooden houses and harvest by hand. Most villages are located on sandy hills, because the valleys flood when the rivers burst their banks. The landscape is hilly, with alternating agricultural land, woods, marshes, lakes, streams and rivers. Everything breathes nature. Belorussia possibly has the highest biodiversity of all European countries. The Berezinski biosphere reserve is an oasis of primeval nature and part of the natural heritage of Belorussia and Europe. The park was set up in 1925 to protect the unique landscape in an area covered with foliage and broadleaved forest and to study the natural processes there. The area has more than 2,000 kinds of vegetation (798 plants, 216 mosses, 463 fungi, 317 algae, 238 lichens), of which 139 are threatened species. The fauna is represented by 52 mammals, 217 species of bird, 10 amphibians, 5 reptiles, 34 species of fish. All European beasts of prey are present. From an ecological point of view swamps and woods are the most important part of the reserve. There are 69 rivers, among them the 110-kilometres-long Berezina, the only river in Belorussia where shipping and the transport of wood are not allowed. There are also 7 lakes, spread over 1,748 hectares.

INTERVIEW WITH FRENCH BIOLOGIST JEAN-CLAUDE GENOT

(Genot is attached to the Vosges du Nord park in France and regularly visits Berezina in connection with international projects for the preservation of nature)

Wolves live close to people here. How is such a symbiosis achieved?

The Berezina region is the only area in Belorussia where the wolf is not hunted. In an area of 86,000 hectares there are twenty to twenty-five wolves. They live close to humans, but the woods and swamps guarantee sufficient space. Moreover, the agricultural activities in the area are diminishing, and the woodland is gaining in territory – a positive development for the wolf. The wolves live mainly in the forested northern region of the area.

Where does this enormous biodiversity – from little owls to elks – come from?

The Berezina region is a patchwork quilt of landscapes: swamps, open peat zones, pine trees, spruce, willows, lakes, watercourses and so on.

What animals can you study here?

The bison, the beaver, the elk, the bear, three species of fowl, the lesser spotted eagle, the osprey, the common crane, the black stork, the white-backed woodpecker, the Ural and the Lapland owls . . .

Why do you keep coming back? What makes Berezina so unique?

I come here for scientific purposes, but also because you can still find pure nature here, which you no longer find in our woods in the Vosges.

What influence could global warming have here?

Global warming could bring on a drought, with the result that the spruce would die off – and possibly disappear altogether. Moreover, on dry subsoil the pine woods could fall victim to forest fires, whether or not started spontaneously, and small watercourses would dry out.

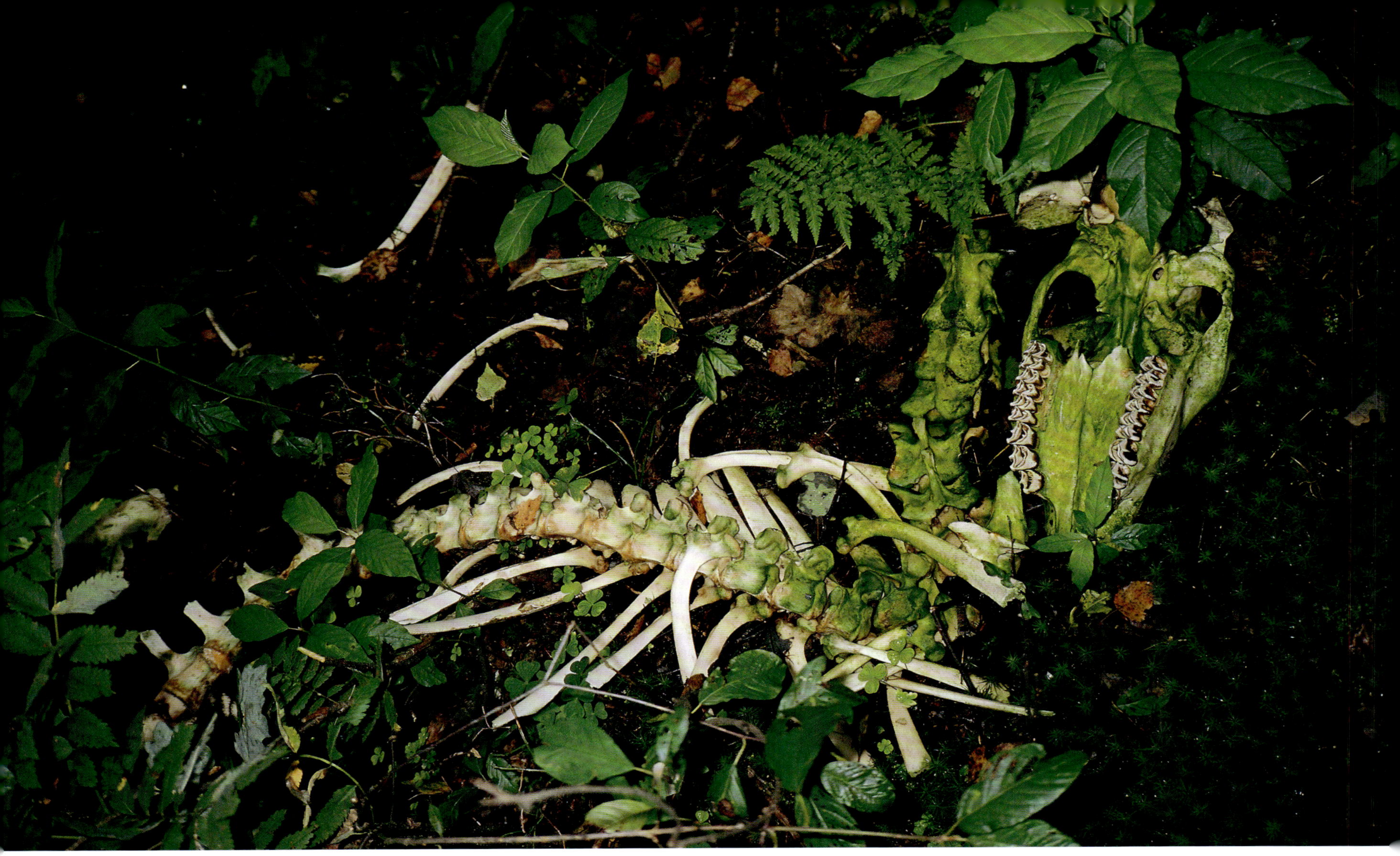

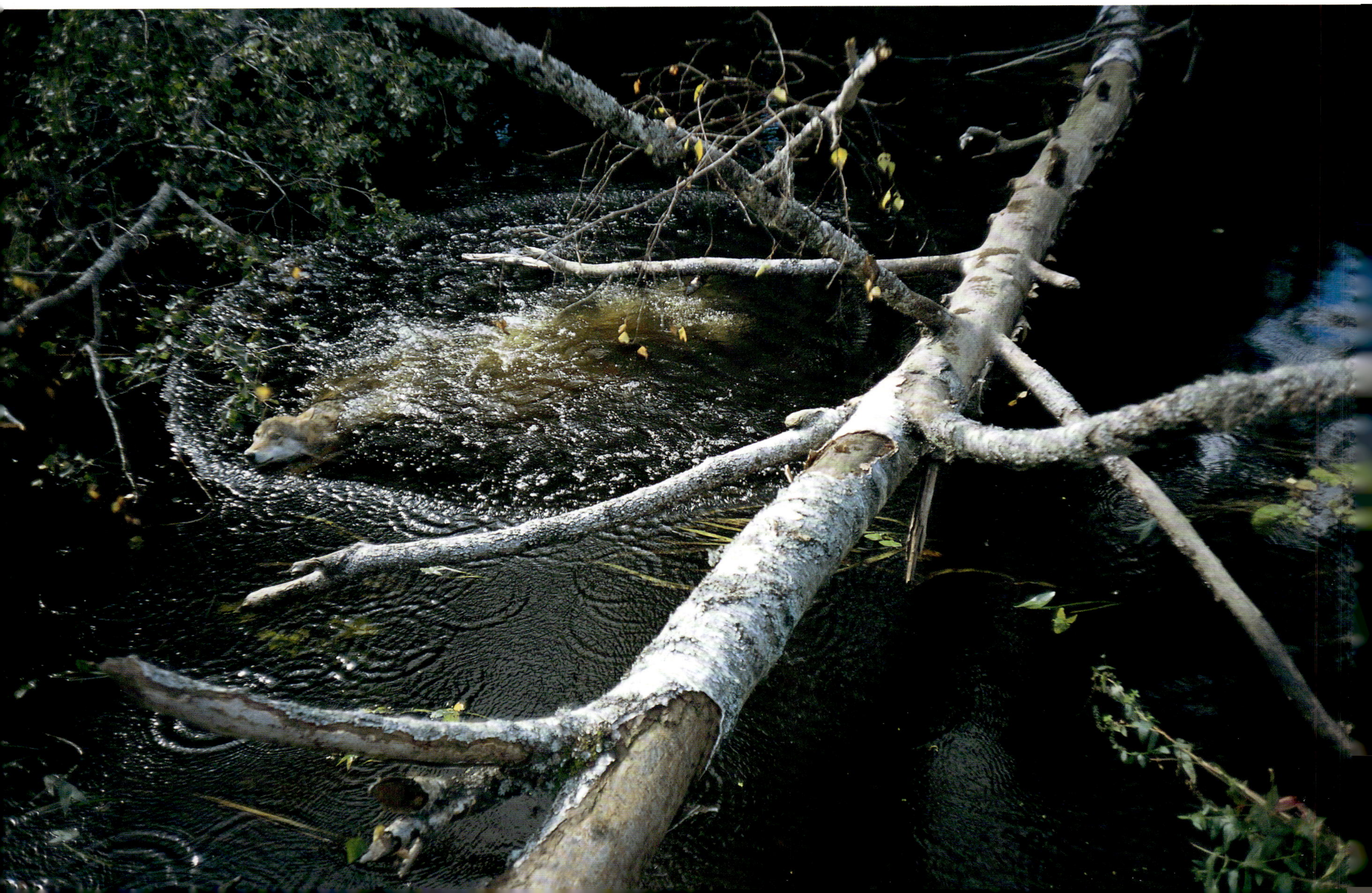

◀ Which predator caused this? As the sun rises the wolf packs howl . . .

◀ Nothing will hold the wolf (Canis lupus) back. In this area Napoleon's armies were brought to a standstill and killed.

▶ Lesser and greater spotted eagles are often seen here. This is where Klimov shot one of the most beautiful Russian films of the last century.

► The goshawk. The birds leave the nest after forty days. They are continually on the alert and behave like pillagers.

► A young goshawk. Its crop is full: the bird is replete. Any animals around can take a short pause for breath.

►► This is the work of a beaver, widely represented in this world of water and marsh.

ACKNOWLEDGMENTS

General scientific advice
Jean-Claude Genot (Park Northern Vosges), Alain Bouchat (biologist), Zjef Pereboom (Antwerp Zoo), Maurice Hoffmann (University of Ghent), Annik Schnitzler (University of Metz), Luc Van Assche (Flemish Agency for Nature and Woodland)

In the field:
Azores: João Rodeia (tourism) Joaquim Teodósio (SPEA, Portuguese Society for the Study of Birds), Rui Prieto (division oceanography University of the Azores)
www.horta.uac.pt/projectos/cetamarh
www.visitazores.org
www.visitportugal.com
Finland: Sanna Kortelainen (Tourism), Tapio Tynys (Lemmenjoki), Sakari Kankaanpaa (Kekkonen)
www.upm-kymmene.com
www.saariselka.fi
www.outdoors.fi
Greece: Irene Koutseri (Prespa), Elena Makrigianni (Evros), Yannis Marinos (WWF Evros)
www.spp.gr
Iceland: Willy Wouters, IJslandreizen (tourism)
www.ijslandreizen.be
www.vreemdekontinenten.be
www.icelandair.be
Italy: Stephano Anile Anile (Etna), Ester Delbove (Basilicata), Lina d'Orazio (Abruzzi), Birgit Van Severen (tourism)
www.boschidisicilia.it,
www.parks.it
www.fondoambiante.it
Norway: Heike Vester (Lofoten), Lex Wagenaar (tourism)
www.visitnorway.com
www.innovasjonnorge.no
www.ocean-sounds.com
Austria: Gunther Gressmann (Hohe Tauern)
www.oostenrijk.be
Poland: Marek Dylawerski (Wolinski), Czeslaw Okolow (Bielowieza), Arthur Wiatr (Biebrza)
www.bpn.com.pl
www.biebrza.org.pl
www.pot.gov.pl
www.wolinpn.pl
Russia: Karev Evgueny (Ural)
Scotland: Mike Daniels (Highlands)
www.jmt.org
Serbia: Dennis van der Avoort (tourism)
www.serbia.travel
www.ndjerdap.org

Slovenia: Dejman
www.slovenia.info
Spain: Luis Fernandez
www.tourspain.es
www.spain.info
www.turismodearagon.com
Turkey: Sinan Ada (Kurdistan)
www.turizm.gov.tr
www.atauni.edu.tr
Portugal: www.visitportugal.com
www.portugalglobal.pt

Photographer's acknowledgments
Erik Verdonck (author), Johan Ghysels (publisher) and Heidi Verschaeve (editor), Jan Mannaert and Hilde Alens (design), Jean-Claude Genot (scientist)

Stavros Dimas (European Commissioner for the Environment), Joke Schauvliege (Flemish Minister for the Environment, Nature & Culture), Paul Magnette (Belgian federal minister of Climate), Joftein Bernhardsen (Norwegian ambassador in Belgium), Aopo Pölho (ambassador of Finland), Akyapi (cultural attaché at the Turkish embassy), Théodore Chartomatsidis, Ulla Suortti, Marret Mattus, Dominica Szule, Eva Konopka, Birgit Vanseveren, Pia Trippia, Rok Klancnik, Dejman, Eva Forstenlechner, Daniela Amico, Robert Joniaux, Danielle Huby, Peter Baldwin, Demesmaker, Dennis Van der Avoort, Dimitry Shamovich, Patrick Fauche, Patricia de Peuter, Willy Wouters, Mario Coppens, Joao Rodeia, Marlène Rocha, Jean-Marie Laloyaux, Ellen Mauritzen, Heleen Notebaert, Eva Podlogar, Amati Corrado, Brigitte Lebleu, Jaques Bulot, Yann Arthus Bertrand

Useful links
General
www.parc-vosges-nord.fr
www.biosphere-vosges
http://pfaelzerwald.org
www.habiterlemondeautrement.com
www.ecology.ugent.be
www.natuurenbos.be
www.kmda.org
http://ec.europa.eu/environment/nature/conservation/species/redlist/#
www.iucnredlist.org
http://ecoagents.eea.europa.eu
http://themes.eea.europa.eu/indicators
www.eea.europa.eu/highlights
www.eea.europa.eu/publications

Ornithology
Tuition in ornithology: www.formation-ornitho.org
The world of ornithology: www.valeryschollaert.com

Frances Lincoln Ltd
4 Torriano Mews
Torriano Avenue
London NW5 2RZ
www.franceslincoln.com

Wild Europe
This English edition copyright © Frances Lincoln 2011
Copyright original Dutch edition © Lannoo Publishers, 2011

First Frances Lincoln edition: 2011

Text: Erik Verdonck and Eric Brasseur
Photography: Eric Brasseur
English translation: Alastair and Cora Weir
Design: Beeld.Inzicht
Cartography: Tatjana Matysik

A catalogue record for this book is available from the British Library.

ISBN 9780711232242